Be the Change in the Hospitality Industry

Rikhsibay Tursunov

Be the Change in the Hospitality Industry
Copyright © 2022 Rikhsibay Tursunov
First published in 2022

Print: 978-1-76124-034-8
E-book: 978-1-76124-035-5
Hardback: 978-1-76124-033-1

All rights reserved. No part of this book may be reproduced, stored in a retrieval system, or transmitted by any means (electronic, mechanical, photocopying, recording, or otherwise) without written permission from the author.

Because of the dynamic nature of the Internet, any web addresses or links contained in this book may have changed since publication and may no longer be valid. The information in this book is based on the author's experiences and opinions. The views expressed in this book are solely those of the author and do not necessarily reflect the views of the publisher; the publisher hereby disclaims any responsibility for them.

The author of this book does not dispense any form of medical, legal, financial, or technical advice either directly or indirectly. The intent of the author is solely to provide information of a general nature to help you in your quest for personal development and growth. In the event you use any of the information in this book, the author and the publisher assume no responsibility for your actions. If any form of expert assistance is required, the services of a competent professional should be sought.

Publishing information
Publishing, design, and production facilitated by Passionpreneur Publishing, A division of Passionpreneur Organization Pty Ltd, ABN: 48640637529

www.PassionpreneurPublishing.com
Melbourne, VIC | Australia

TABLE OF CONTENTS

Introduction	v
Dedication	ix
Acknowledgements	xi
Why My Book Is Good for You	1
My Story	9
Chapter 3 Introduction	15
Early Life and Childhood	17
Chapter 4 Introduction	31
Creating a Great First Impression	33
Chapter 5 Introduction	73
Reinventing the Recruiting Wheel	75
Chapter 6 Introduction	105
Developing Future Leaders	107

Chapter 7 Introduction	139
The Future of Hospitality	141
Last few words	159
Testimonials	163
Author's Bio	169

INTRODUCTION

Being able to learn how to create an emotional connection, harness emotional intelligence and build a strong relationship with everyone we meet, are the top three areas that require a high level of growth. Especially during a time where it is increasingly lacking in various industries across the world. Being in the hospitality industry, where we are all constantly interacting with guests and different background daily, creates an even greater need for these skills to be present. I often get asked by individuals how I maintain such a positive outlook in life and how I can build a strong connection with people. As you read this book, you will be exposed to multiple answers and childhood stories which will help you connect the dots to answer those two main questions mentioned. Emotional intelligence is an asset that all leaders need to sharpen and consistently develop so that their team can be effortlessly encouraged and supported.

This book is for anyone who is looking to develop their emotional intelligence whether they are a student, graduate, employee or curious to enter the hospitality industry. The five key takeaways of the book will help prepare:

1. Students, graduates, and candidates stand out within an interview and make them feel confident as they walk through the door.
2. Recruiters to adopt a different mindset and reinvent their hiring process so that they can detect which candidates are highly driven, passionate, and emotionally intelligent.
3. Leaders to develop their future talent and show them how they can contribute to the current young generation so that they are well prepared when they enter the hospitality industry.
4. Individuals understand what it takes to create a team that is highly compassionate, dedicated, and happy within their work environment.
5. Higher management to support their employee's growth and develop reliable leaders who will be prepared to undertake greater responsibility.

These are the five main areas that will be covered throughout the book and there is a lot for everyone to learn. I want to share my stories, the struggles that I have been through and what I have adopted over the years because it can help anyone who reads this to create a health work environment that is filled with a dedicated, happy, and loyal team. Everyone wants to find out how to keep their team consistently motivated, how to achieve incredible results and ultimately become successful. This book offers every single reader the tools that can help them achieve greater emotional intelligence, better human connection, and a higher sense of understanding. These tools that I am sharing with you are my own methods that I have come up with throughout the experiences that I have undergone and now I want to pass them on to you so that they can be just as useful. Coming up with these methods and tools has been an ongoing process, and it all started early on during my childhood. So let me take you through this journey as I start sharing where it all began.

DEDICATION

I would like to dedicate this book to my entire family, but most importantly my mother. Her continuous positive outlook on life, unconditional love and encouraging support is what truly helped shape my character at such a young age. These crucial building blocks made the difference and gave me the confidence that anything is possible if I believe in it and work hard towards it. Without her help, I would not have accomplished even half of what I currently have. My strong and supportive upbringing, no matter the financial situation, is all thanks to her.

ACKNOWLEDGEMENTS

I would like to express my gratitude to every single encounter that I ever had with everyone throughout my life. Without those interactions, learnings, twists, and turns, I would not be the same person I am today. I believe that every single event and scenario is there for a reason and teaches us something.

1

WHY MY BOOK IS GOOD FOR YOU

Growing up as a curious kid, I was always excited to discover something new, and as soon as I came up with a new idea, I wanted to test it out. Ideas for businesses always sprouted in my imagination as I interacted with different people and observed daily life.

When I first started working to help support my parents, I would try to learn and get guidance from people that had already worked in that field. I often found myself seeking advice from these intelligent people, but they were always too busy or stuck in their own little bubble, working hard to survive. They were unable to make time to teach me the ropes of life or guide me to follow my career path. Growing up in this environment was different for me.

Despite not being able to lean on others for knowledge, I had my mother, who was extremely positive and encouraging. I call her my hero because she constantly pushed me and guided me to follow my dreams. She was the one who put me on the right track and helped me build strong habits that later supported my career path.

Now that I have acquired years of experience and reached this senior level, I want to be the person who goes out of their way to offer guidance, advice, and help to anyone who needs it, without them asking me first. I try to make knowledge accessible to all the people who are curious enough to seek it. This is about being able to make a difference in people's lives.

I need to share the knowledge that I have learned over the past 25 years because everyone needs someone who can inspire them to take that risk, guide them towards their dream, or teach them something new. This is the main reason I started to write this book, to impact the world by offering new solutions within the hospitality industry and ultimately leave a legacy for the new generation.

Becoming a role model for my children and the young generation is very close to my heart. There are multiple individuals out there who have incredible stories, knowledge, and lessons to share with the world, but they find it extremely difficult to do so. I believe that once everyone shares their struggles, learnings, and endeavours, it can help others learn.

When we share, we ultimately feel happier and more positive. However, not everyone is comfortable becoming this vulnerable and that's because they either fear other people's judgements, they do not feel comfortable sharing their past shortcomings or they do not want to be replaced by someone who can do their job better than them. I strongly believe that only by sharing our wisdom can the future generation learn from our mistakes and lessons and become even more successful than us.

I realised that my passion lies in human connection and helping people. Every day when I wake up, I always ask myself, 'I wonder how many times I can make people smile throughout the day?'. I never have a specific number in mind, I mainly know that I want to brighten up people's day and give them a reason to smile and be happy. That is why I always start conversations with different people; they could be people who are working on the streets in 40-degree Celsius weather, people who are driving taxis all around the city or anyone who shares the same elevator with me.

My interest in starting conversations with people and being curious about who they are has led me to understand them better. This is a deeply rooted habit that stemmed from my desire to connect with people from a young age. Now, this same habit has given me the power to understand people of all cultures, backgrounds, religions, and nationalities. Ever since I started to strengthen my cultural awareness, it was easy for me to analyse the environment of a room filled with people and transform any negative conversations into positive ones. Within the hospitality industry, it's extremely important to create an amicable environment where diverse team members can peacefully coexist and work to succeed together. This is an important aspect that falls under crisis management and building the foundations of strong company culture.

Trying to run multiple business ideas when I was younger not only helped me learn how to connect with individuals, but it also gave me a taste of knowing when to take a risk, how to make good decisions and being time efficient. Currently, multiple leaders wait to reach the 95 per cent certainty threshold before making a decision, however, if I am 60 per cent sure that an idea will work then I will execute it without any hesitation. This process will reveal if the idea does or doesn't work, but in the end, we are still able to move forward because there is always something to learn from the outcome. When it does work, it teaches us that we need to take more risks as there's always a higher chance of achieving something as long as we try. When the idea does not work, then we learn why it didn't and we look to understand how we can do things differently. Repeating this process helps practice the habit of improving confidence by stepping into the unknown and teaches us to push fear away when the unknown appears.

Usually, people have an innate fear of taking risks and I often find myself offering people mentorship and guidance to help them gain confidence in what they truly want to achieve. Over the past 25 years, I have come to realise that whether people reach out to me or not, I often mentor people and keep them inspired and hopeful.

A common topic that people want to learn about is how they can create a genuine and authentic human connection with others. Connection, leadership, and emotional intelligence are three pillars within the hospitality industry that I find myself teaching others. This is mainly because I asm good at inspiring people and giving them the confidence to go to the next level. At the same time, I am also great at mentoring people and creating a positive work environment through my leadership skills and emotional intelligence. The main way I can contribute to the hospitality industry is through using my emotional intelligence to help others create a cohesive working environment in the hospitality industry.

This book is for future and current hospitality leaders from around the world who want to make a difference and be the change in the hospitality industry—the leaders who want to understand the importance of human connection and how to achieve it in their workforce. In the end, it's the positive and influential leader who can shape the company's values. When colleagues genuinely believe, respect and trust in the company's new culture, they will feel connected enough to embrace the new changes and support their leader in their new visions. I can be the one who can help you, the hospitality industry leader, to embed emotional intelligence within day-to-day processes that will ultimately help transform your team's work culture and help build true human connections.

The way I do this is simple and is customised to every hotel or company because there is a unique story everywhere. My standard process for emotional intelligence integration is as follows:

1. **Analysis** – This is the part where I observe a company's culture and background by interacting with various employees, managers, and supervisors during their daily tasks. This involves speaking with them and getting to know them better.
2. **Review** – Once a deep understanding is achieved, it will be easier for me to paint a full picture of the interconnection of the different departments and find out their connection percentage.
3. **Identify** – Merging the analysis and review aspect gives rise to the identification of different areas of growth.
4. **Blueprint** – Once the areas of growth are identified, I will be able to create a customised blueprint that will act as the main plan of action.

This process will help you, the leader, to create a happy work environment that will inspire your colleagues and employees to work towards a unified goal. An environment that adopts empathy and emotional intelligence will cultivate individuals who want to continually learn and grow. Currently, it is not common to find a leader who has climbed the ladder of various stages in the hospitality industry.

Having worked in multiple positions and levels within a hotel, I have observed and learned how to identify the obstacles and issues that various colleagues go through. This is an extremely important skill that not everyone has. Having extensive knowledge about the operations processes gives me the ability to deeply understand the various issues that appear in daily procedures.

By reading my book, I hope to share my knowledge and expertise to be able to take you to the next level. This leads me to offer you a glimpse of how I leapt into the hospitality industry by moving to the United Arab Emirates, and what it took to adapt to this new environment. This environment was different from any I'd ever known.

2

MY STORY

Moving to another country for the first time, away from family, friends, and the support system that you have built and grown accustomed to is always difficult. It introduces multiple challenges that you would not have otherwise thought of, ranging from new cultures, traditions, customs, religions, and nationalities of people.

For me, the start of my hospitality journey abroad started with moving to Dubai after a former manager recommended and hired me to be part of the team. Throughout my entire childhood and young adult life, it was extremely important for me to help support my family and introduce them to a better way of life. Despite travelling and moving into the unknown, I knew that it was the change that I needed to grow, learn, and open new doors of opportunities. It was scary not knowing what lay ahead because it was the first time I was going to a place where I did not know anyone, the first time travelling on my own outside of my country and the first time I would step on a plane.

As I sat on the plane, it really started to sink in that I was moving away from my family, the people who had been there for me my entire life and who had always encouraged me to follow all my ideas. As I was flying towards this new chapter of my life, I started to panic, and fear started to settle in my mind. It is normal to be scared whenever we try something new and unfamiliar, but the most important part is being able to overcome that fear. At that moment, I knew that I had to ground myself and remember my vision, purpose, and why I decided to leave the comfort of my home. Remembering that this was for my family and personal growth is what kept me going.

Most importantly, it was the advice that my grandmother shared with me that helped keep me grounded. This was a day before I left when family, relatives and close friends gathered to share my favourite meal before I departed. It was a day filled with celebration, long conversations, and a bitter-sweet departure. As I went to wish my grandmother the best and to tell her I was soon going to leave, she told me three important things that I still carry with me in my heart to this day. She told me that I could never forget our culture and the way we were brought up: very family-oriented, humble and extremely supportive of everyone, no matter who they are and wherever they are from. She explained to me that as soon as I land in the United Arab Emirates, I needed to be humble and show respect to every single individual, regardless of how small or big their role or position was. The final thing she told me was to become adaptive to that culture and be open to understanding every single person, where they come from, what they value, and what they like. These three highly important pieces of wisdom were carried in my heart and mind, in every step I took, whether it was when I interacted with customers, colleagues, or the higher management. In a way, my grandmother's wisdom became the leading pillar of my life as I began my journey in a foreign place that I now consider my second home.

Back then I had no idea the impact this country would have on my growth professionally and personally. That is why I am extremely grateful that the UAE has welcomed me with open arms and care, allowing me to follow my passion and supporting my dreams of changing the hospitality scene by introducing a greater connection between individuals.

The first three areas that posed great difficulty for me related to building new habits I was not used to, proving myself in a new environment, and being surrounded by a lack of excitement. Firstly, building new habits encompassed welcoming different ways of living. This meant I had to become accustomed to the different backgrounds of people as we were around 25 different nationalities within the workforce, and everyone was carrying their background and culture as a proud badge. The food and environment that I was suddenly a part of were completely different from what I was used to back home. Initially, this created a sense of isolation for me and I naturally cried a few times at night at the end of my day. Every single time I would remind myself why I was there and what my main purpose was. That constant reminder is what truly kept me grounded when faced with any difficulty and my grandmother's wise words would constantly echo in my mind. I then worked to understand people, respect them, and make them feel heard whenever we would converse. This not only allowed them to feel listened to and important, but it opened the door for them to become friendly and open to sharing ideas and understanding our different backgrounds. Through the concept of being seen and heard, one or two of us were able to create a family bond.

It took some time to win the acceptance of everyone else, especially since many of them believed that I was working there just because of my long-standing connection with one of the higher management managers. This was not true, and I had to work extremely hard to prove that my position within the company was based purely on the talent and skill set that I brought to the working environment. Conversing with multiple people throughout the day, mostly through small talk and gestures because I was still developing my English, helped me to understand every single customer we had. Paying attention to the small details, such as remembering a customer's favourite breakfast meals, bringing them their preferred coffee without being told to do so, and greeting them with a huge smile on my face every single time we met, made me stand out. At the time I was not aware, and I was just working to do my best for our customers. Going the extra mile was reflected three months later when I was given a certificate of congratulations by the hotel management in recognition of my excellent service over six months from October 2001 to March 2002. The feedback was compiled from multiple guest questionnaires during that timeframe and reflected a significant effort in making guests feel welcome. I was slowly becoming known as one of the highly successful employees because of my incredible ratings and mentions. This surprised most of the staff members present because I was new to the hotel and many of them had the misconception that I was only there because of my connection to the manager. As I worked harder and harder, this misconception dissolved, and people were naturally drawn to me so that they could also learn and improve in their designated jobs. It was not easy making these moves and constantly maintaining the positivity along the way, however, to understand where I got this burst of positivity and drive, we need to go back in time to my childhood. That is where I truly built those habits, values, and ways of thinking. In the next chapter, I will give you a little insight into my life before moving to the UAE. There, I hope you will be able to identify the life lessons that I went through and apply them to your life.

CHAPTER 3 INTRODUCTION

This is a chapter that is close to my heart – most people have not heard all the stories that I am about to reveal, and that's only one part of what makes this book special. These are the series of events that have had a tremendous impact on moulding me into the person I am today. Everything from my values to my habits stems from these experiences. The way our mentality forms and the habits that we built when we are young is crucial to building a strong foundation that will ultimately help us climb to greater heights. I would say that this chapter is dedicated to my mother, a woman whose resilience, strength and power turned the entire family into true fighters and taught me that anything is achievable. She would pour buckets of positivity every morning as soon as I opened my eyes 'til my sleepy head landed on my pillow at night. She injected this sense of confidence into my personality every time she supported me in all my crazy business ideas. And for that, I will be more than thankful for the rest of my life.

This one is for you, Mum.

3

EARLY LIFE AND CHILDHOOD

We all know how important the first stage of our life is. More specifically, our youth. At that age we are like sponges, ready to soak up every new experience or learn something different. The mind is curious, adventurous, and on the lookout for something different. We still haven't encountered or adapted to the "What If" mentality that prevents many people from chasing their childhood dream or burning passion. Let's look at it this way, the same thing happens when it comes to learning a new language. Why do you think children find it easier to learn multiple languages when they are young, as opposed to when they grow up? It's because they are not afraid to make mistakes or to speak to others in another language. Unshakeable confidence and a sense of encouragement overtake their system.

Over time, as children grow into teenagers and then into adults, negativity, failures, or bad experiences tend to break the orb of possibility that individually surrounds them. This is not an irreversible outcome as people decide to work on reclaiming their confidence. I often get asked how I have managed to carry this confidence and positive mindset throughout my youth and into adulthood. Despite a tough upbringing – as you will soon find out – confidence and positivity remained untainted.

Growing up in the countryside of Uzbekistan, I was the only boy alongside my three sisters and my parents. When my uncle, unfortunately, passed away at a young age, my three cousins did not have a father anymore. That is how my three sisters became six and our family became even bigger. From a young age, this instilled a strong sense of responsibility in me because I always felt like I needed to protect them all. We were lucky enough to share two rooms between the five of us and my cousins, along with their mother, lived with my grandmother in another house. One room was used as a dining room where we would all gather to eat together. The other room was used by myself, my sisters, and my mother to sleep. My father would normally sleep in the same room where we all ate. Seeing my father sleeping in the same room where we ate made my heart feel heavy and sent a signal that I would need to do something to change this. We could not possibly live like this forever, especially since we did not have a proper roof over our heads. I mean, we had a ceiling, but the roof was not fully constructed. We were lucky to own this space only because it was given to us by my grandmother who lived right next to us in her small house. It was a tight fit for us all but at the time there wasn't any other option. The majority of the days when I would open our fridge to see if something had changed, I would be greeted by the same vegetables – onions and potatoes. We had a few chickens in the backyard so I would be able to pick the fresh eggs. I would mainly cook potatoes, with eggs and finely chopped onions. Funnily enough, this is still my favourite meal today even though now our fridge at home is fully stocked with different types of food.

From an early age, I started to have a burning desire to start making my own money so that I could help the family and start buying my own clothes without having to feel like a burden. I was constantly on the lookout, trying to observe how everyone else in town was making money to survive and how they made sure they could provide for the family. That's how my young business adventures began. From the age of fourteen to sixteen, I was jumping through various ventures, trying to replicate the businesses that worked across town. There are four main stories that I will be sharing with you so that you can see what I have learned from them and how they have shaped me.

1. Building the habit of being patient

It was an extremely early morning and I happened to be awake. It might have been as early as five o'clock because the rooster started to sing, and the birds began to chirp. This usually only happened at sunrise. As I looked outside our window, I saw our next-door neighbour walk around carrying a huge container. An instant wave of curiosity washed over me; I needed to know what was in that container and where he was going. I ran outside to catch up with him and find out.

He was in a rush, but I managed to find out that he was going to sell fresh Samsa at the animal market. Samsa is popular in Uzbekistan and can be easily described as a small triangular pastry that is filled with vegetables and meat. It is also drizzled with either sesame seeds or nigella seeds. Selling Samsa at the animal market sounded like a really good way to make money. That same morning, I decided to announce to the whole family that I would also be selling Samsa at the animal market.

My mother initially said, 'But, you've never been to the animal market before!' I told her that it wouldn't be a problem because I could easily go one day and learn. Since then, I began to visit my neighbour more often. We would sit together and talk for at least half an hour every day. This was my way of building a good relationship and following my curiosity so that maybe one day I could visit the animal market with him.

After a couple of days, I was invited to go with him and see how it all worked. We had to wake up early because the animal market would usually start their daily sales at five o'clock and by nine o'clock in the morning, most of the people would slowly disappear. The highest quality farm animals were always bought at the earliest hour so I needed to make sure that we would be present when a lot of people were visiting. As we arrived at the animal market, I was hit with the strong stench of manure from all the cows, horses, and goats. While I was walking, my shoes would sink halfway into the mud mixed with the manure. I could not believe we were making our way to the middle of the animal market. My neighbour said that we need to set up there because that's where all the people came to eat and to purchase the livestock.

I accompanied my neighbour for a total of two days and during that time I was also able to sell some Samsa because he left me in charge of the stand for 30 minutes as he went to fetch us some drinking water. I was able to absorb every single second, looking at how people interacted and how they responded. We were at the epicentre of the trade hub; we were surrounded by loud people negotiating and haggling to get the cheapest prices for the best animals.

After seeing that I was able to do this on my own, I went home to tell my family about my experience. It was my second sister who insisted we could also make this happen. For the next four weeks, my sisters and my mum would wake up at four o'clock in the morning to bake the Samsas and arrange them neatly in a container for me. I would then take them to the market while they were still hot and fresh. Samsa is the type of dish that is best eaten when it is freshly baked, and everyone at the animal market knew this. It's what made me stand out because others would cook or bake them the previous night and the food would not taste as good. I always looked for ways to stand out to sell my products.

That is why I would be one of the few who would shout and sing "Come get your fresh Samsa, baked this morning, they are still hot." You had to fight for attention in the animal market, especially since everyone was already there with their own purpose and agenda. Being surrounded by the atrocious smell of the animals' droppings made it difficult to breathe properly. It was a challenge to keep myself composed so that I would not vomit. In the end, I did not care where I was as long as I was able to make my own money. My main motivation to keep going was my family. That is why every morning once I finished selling the Samsas at the market, I would make sure to go buy bread or vegetables so that I could bring them back home. This experience taught me the true meaning of being patient and building resilience even when I was surrounded by the worst physical conditions.

Multiple times in life we are faced with difficult or uncomfortable situations. However, the more we endure these situations for the greater benefit, the better we build our habit of having patience and resilience in tough situations. In the end, these uncomfortable situations don't last forever. They are temporary, but our learning is eternal. Adapting to the moment was the second lesson that I learned during this time. It is extremely important to understand that when we place ourselves in unfavourable circumstances, it truly builds our habit of going forward no matter the obstacles we are faced with. In the end, when we overcome these difficulties and are successful in achieving our vision, we build resilience too. Whenever you want to achieve something, you need to have a strong belief system in place that pushes you to remain consistent. That's what differentiates successful people and the rest of the people.

2. Being confident at a young age

Every month I would make my way to my maternal grandmother's house to deliver some medicine. She lost her vision and needed our support in getting the right medication. Since she lived on the outskirts of the other side of the village, I would have to pass by different roads and highways on the way. There was this specific road that really grabbed my attention because whenever I passed by, I saw the opportunity and potential of trying out a new business idea.

This was a road that was heavily trafficked by big cargo trucks and trailers. Normally, they would stop on the side of the road to buy snacks and drinks as they took a break. This was why this area was filled with different women on the side of the road with their wooden tables. They would sell different snacks, sweets, soft drinks, and juices that the drivers would stop and buy. One day I decided that I would also try to do the same, so I went to the supermarket to buy some soft drinks. I did not have enough money to buy a lot and I was not able to carry a lot on my own. That was why I was only able to afford to buy 48 bottles of soft drinks which would last for roughly two days. I would make my way to that specific roadside and set up my stand next to everyone else. I had never sold fizzy drinks on the side of the road before, but I knew that I had to be the first to grab the attention of truck drivers that passed by. To do this, I decided to move my stand and set up half a meter in front of everyone else.

It was no surprise that this worked and the other older ladies who were selling their own produce noticed this too. They started to get a bit frustrated about this since customers would buy from me.

Some of the women started to shout at me, "who do you think you are, coming here?" or "we have been here a lot longer than you have", or "we've been in the business longer than you, what are you doing here anyway?".

Being there despite my young age and the intimidation that I felt being surrounded by other people who were in the business longer than I have me the confidence to never give up just because I am new at something. At times it is normal for someone to feel like they do not belong there because they do not have the status or experience. My advice is to constantly try something, even if you are new at it because you never know how you can do things differently or sometimes even better than others.

3. Sell or starve – the tale of self-taught discipline

Another side hustle that I used to undertake when I was fourteen years old was selling vegetables at the bazaar. This entire process took determination and taught me that I needed to follow a certain schedule and reach a certain target to become successful.

My mornings would start with waking up extremely early to rush and purchase the vegetables in bulk from wholesalers.

This meant that I needed to be present at the truck's meet-up point at five o'clock in the morning to get my hands on the best-looking produce before everyone else did. Then I would make my way to the bazaar to set everything up and make it look presentable for all the customers. By nine o'clock I would have already polished, cleaned and arranged all the vegetables. My interactions with people would have finally started and would only end in the evening by four o'clock. I would always make a promise to myself that if I sold at least 80 per cent of the produce that I bought then I would allow myself to have lunch. If I did not reach my target by the end of the evening, then I would deprive myself of lunch. I wanted to sell everything on the same day that I bought it because I wanted everything to be fresh for the customers. Nothing was to be brought home, and everything had to be sold so that I would succeed in making enough profit. This was my way of practising self-disciplining and it taught me that I can celebrate once I achieved the goals that set out to complete. The hard part of this process was remaining positive and confident no matter the outcome during that day. You cannot be positive one day and be down the next. I had to apply positivity to my consistent discipline. I kept reminding myself that if I failed, no one would be there to earn extra money for the family. It was up to me to keep going and maintain that consistency no matter what.

4. How insects helped me make money

I was always looking for new opportunities to earn some quick extra cash. I believe that there is always an opportunity for someone to learn or earn something extra, it just takes an open mindset – a mindset that is searching for something new.

One day when I was walking home from school, I was approached by the supervisor who worked at a government-owned farm. He asked me if I was interested in being paid for an easy job. All I had to do was help clean the potato field from insects that were destroying the plants. At the time, I could not believe that a bottle filled with those insects would pay me 25 Roubles. That was a considerable amount back then and it was an easy way to earn cash. I decided to accept the job since it was performed only through manual labour, and they did not have the pesticides available to kill the insects.

It was an extremely difficult process because it was smelly and disgusting. However, I did not let that stop me. I signed and wrote down my name so that I would be contacted once the pay arrived. Every day I would go back to the guard to ask him whether the money arrived. After two or three months of constantly checking in, just as I was about to give up, I was told that the pay finally arrived, and I could collect it. This taught me that I should never feel too proud to do any job and that if something needs to be done, no matter how much I hate the process, I should push myself to do it.

In life, we are going to encounter unpleasant scenarios that we do not agree with. The most important part of dealing with these situations is how we react and if we embrace them with a positive attitude as we focus on the outcome. Just like the insect-picking process was not permanent, any unpleasant scenario in your life is also not permanent.

5. Afraid to ask for help?

Plenty of people are afraid to ask for help or struggle with the fear of being perceived as 'inexperienced' or 'incompetent'. I believe that our curiosity and drive to learn are some of the strongest powers and tools that we can use. In the end, we are all life-long learners and there will always be something new to learn. This ultimately gives us the push to grow and evolve in either our studies, career or personal life.

I learned from a young age to ask for help and to seek out answers to my questions. Growing up, I had the support of my parents, but I did not have guidance from professors or industry professionals, especially at the tender ages between fourteen and sixteen. That was why I went out on my own to get answers to questions I was curious about.

There was a specific bus stop area where there were wooden stands that were accompanied by individuals who would sell snacks and drinks. This stand was run by two men, and they were also set up in four to five different key locations across town. I wanted to learn how they managed their little street shops and how they made everything work. It was easy for me to approach them and ask them if I could work with them for free just to learn. They were more than happy to teach me and even gave me a trial period for a week. This gave me enough time to gain all the knowledge I needed to set up my own table beautifully. During the upcoming summer, I continued to set up my own table and I even hired my friend as an employee to help me manage the area. That way it was easy for me to roam around the city and look for more opportunities. I may have not been able to rent a place, but I was still able to manage my own stand at the bus stop.

CHAPTER 4 INTRODUCTION

By now you can see that I did not really have an easy childhood where I would join the other kids to play outside or stay out late with friends. I had to grow up and mature a little quicker than everyone else and during that time, I had to find my own way to navigate life. Multiple people have role models they look up to, but I did not really hold anyone in high regard. Mentorship and guidance were two concepts that were foreign to me when growing up, and I constantly had to go looking for answers myself. I was not really prepared for interviews – I didn't know what to say. I mainly had to believe in myself and just do my best on the spot. Now that I have undergone multiple experiences, I want to share them. That's why through the next chapter, I will be sharing advice and tips on how you can prepare for an interview, stand out during an interview, and different ways to build networks.

4

CREATING A GREAT FIRST IMPRESSION

Being fresh out of high school or university makes multiple students realise the true meaning of stepping into the real world where they need to start 'adulting'. Like many other graduates, this step feels like the most important one in life because, having just graduated, many young minds have an eagerness to change the world and make a difference with their big ideas, but at the same time a lot of overpowering pressure from the competition can arise. With time, it slowly becomes apparent that contrary to what multiple people were brought up to believe, knowledge and education are not everything. The realisation that there is more to education than theory, and that on-the-job experience is extremely fundamental to success starts to settle. Experience and learning on the job become a lot more important since one of the best ways to learn is through mentorship and guidance.

The three main aspects that are extremely important in helping kick-start a career in the hospitality industry in early youth years are: making your CV stand out, creating an impact during your interview process, and becoming memorable throughout your working period. This is exactly what chapter four will address.

When I was growing up, I did not have anyone to guide me and to tell me, "Rikhsibay this is what you should do to get this job", "Rikhsibay, it's passion and purpose that will make you feel like you are not even working when you are working", "This is what you need to keep doing to gain trust and recognition", or even, "this is how you build a strong professional relationship where you are valued". I had none of that guidance, and on top of that, I did not go down the traditional university degree path. Instead, I went to a vocational college where I learned about the tourism and hospitality industry for three-quarters of the time and the rest of the time I was interning while simultaneously earning money through my side businesses. This chapter is extremely important for me because I want to share my advice and successful tactics which can help create greater clarity and guidance around anyone's early stages of their hospitality career. All these different formulas and successful tactics took me years of experimenting, risk-taking, and embracing what then felt like scary and unknown experiences, to form what works best. Compiling all this knowledge creates an even greater inner desire to share it with the current youth because, in the end, those are the future leaders. So firstly, let's start with how someone can stand out through their CV.

Making your CV stand out in a massive pool of applicants

Throughout the year, the hospitality industry embraces its very own seasonal spikes in job applications. Various young individuals who are eager to kick-start their career apply for a myriad of opportunities, hoping to land at least a couple of interviews. During this time, recruiters are also on the lookout for their next brilliant team that would best fit their culture, vision, and direction to ultimately achieve their long-term growth and goals.

With thousands and thousands of applicants hoping to secure an interview for either their desired internship or entry-level position, the recruiter's inboxes overflow with prospective candidates. This grand influx of emails can easily result in recruiters skimming through CVs, or as I like to call it the 'professional provisional history', to shortlist final candidates.

And let's face it, quite often, these CVs are not fully read, and sometimes they are not given the attention they deserve.

Presently, the typical construction of a CV includes the education certification, previous experiences, achievements, contact details and top skills if there is enough space to fit everything on one page. With multiple applicants sharing similar aspects, how can you be the one to stand out? What makes you different from everyone else? This competitive drive to show up as unique and as authentic as possible is in everyone's mind.

There are five main ways to make your CV stand out. Firstly, you must be very honest about the work experience presented in your CV because you could possibly be called in for an interview. When those questions start to roll, you need to be able to answer them truthfully. If you think 'winging it' can help you, it truly might help you get your foot in the door but sooner or later, this gap will eventually surface. Admitting that you have gaps in your knowledge but that you are willing to learn speaks for the type of character you have. It shows that you are a curious individual who is willing to adapt and become flexible when presented with new challenges.

This is precisely what leaders look for when acquiring new talent because it is easier to mould someone enthusiastic about adding new skills to their toolbox, rather than someone who wants to do everything their way. Honesty will help anyone garner more support because at the end of the day every single person knows how hard it was to kick-start their career, and if they are a true leader, they will appreciate the honesty. Otherwise, if you are dishonest, you might become part of a team that needs to rely heavily on you, but you will not be able to truly give your best since you still have gaps in your capabilities. Sooner or later these gaps will begin to materialise, and it will be harder to gain the trust of your colleagues and superiors.

Secondly, it is important to mention if you worked somewhere for a month or two, or if you have completed any sort of small job before during your university or college years. Any extracurricular activity that is outside the scope of studies reflects your ability to be able to manage your time wisely.

The third component is the content that you place in your CV. As I mentioned, the current norm is to include your picture, past experiences, achievements, and education in your CV, however, what if you include a small part about your childhood? You might be wondering, "but what does my past or childhood have to do with the current job that I am applying for?". It has everything to do with applying for a new job or internship. It creates a deeper understanding of the person who is behind this CV, and it introduces a better connection to the recruiter. This childhood story could be a memory of how you turned the living room of your house into a hotel dining experience for your family, where you were the chef and waiter during the family's Saturday morning breakfast. It could be a story about a small business or a side project that you went out of your way to set up. These small stories introduce greater empathy and reflect the type of person that you are.

A CV can never truly highlight your personality or the type of person that you are, but these small little stories are a window into your personality and character. Within the hospitality industry character, the way you interact with colleagues, guests and managers is extremely important. That is why if you can share even one small story that can highlight the type of person you are, then you will be more likely to be picked for the interview process.

In this fast-paced world where the fourth industrial revolution is currently heavily underway, technology plays a huge role in our day-to-day lives. The youth is more embedded in the virtual world than ever before, which is more of a reason to share stories that include elements of genuine human connection.

Another way to stand out after applying for a specific role is by going a step further than anyone else. Let me use this phrase that parents have been using for a long time: Back in my day we did not have the technology to send our experience through email from the comfort of our small home. If anyone wanted to apply for a position, they would have to physically go to that place and make sure the correct person received the application. During this time, applications could have also been misplaced or overlooked, and that is why it is extremely important to follow up with recruiters. In my time, it was physically misplaced but presently your CV can be just as well hidden within the large pool of applicants because of the thousands of emails we receive daily! These emails are on top of the usual business- and work-related emails.

One way to follow up and take a step further than everyone else is by visiting the hotel or restaurant that you have applied to. How many times have you applied and just relied on hearing a response through email? It has become a norm to rely on technology, however, despite technology making our lives easier, it also hides the type of people that we are. Behind the online coverage, social media posts and the CVs we send out, we all have a unique personality and character which we are only able to show once we meet with people. Only once we can have a couple of conversations can truly gauge the type of person someone is. That is why it is extremely important to try and reach out to the place you have applied to. Drive to their offices, take a taxi to the hotel, get a friend to drop you off, ask your parents or take the metro! But show up in their lobby and ask how you can speak to the manager or supervisor that is on duty. Start a conversation with their staff members and slowly make your way up the chain. Do whatever it takes to show up and be present. It can seem scary and uncomfortable because it is not something that is presently acknowledged as common practice, but that is exactly why you should do it. Showing up reflects your courage, your go-getter attitude and it makes you memorable since most of the applicants do not think of going a step further like this.

If you are not able to go there physically, why not create a short one-minute video explaining why you applied for this role, how you can bring value to the company and why you believe you are the best fit for the role. Transform that cover letter into a video and send it alongside your CV. A greater connection is built when the recruiter can see who you are and when they get to know you more personally. We are all much more than what fits on a single sheet of A4 paper. Attach a link to your video that is uploaded either through WeTransfer or Vimeo in the email copy rather than within the CV itself. This way you make sure it does not get overlooked within the CV. Since the A4 space is limiting, you can also include QR codes within the one-pager which links recruiters to websites or projects that you have completed.

Creating your own website to act as your very own online portfolio is another way to go the extra mile. Every corner of your website might not be viewed by the recruiter, however, it speaks loudly about the effort you are willing to make, and sometimes that is exactly what matters. Team members who are willing to go the extra mile to support the team and help when no one else is willing to. This foreshadows your ability to be reliable.

Now, let's look at the other side of the story. Let's say you apply to ten different companies, but you never get a reply. This is a likely scenario that you will face at some stage in your life, and you must be prepared for it. During this time, it is important to reach out and find out why you have not been contacted. This will give you guidance for how you can improve in the future or at least give you an insight into what additional skills were required. You will not always be able to get this feedback since some recruiters are not reachable or they may not make time for it. This can lead to frustration and your interest level might go down. That is why it is important not to drift into negative thoughts that can temporarily attack your confidence. Your qualifications and capabilities are not determined by a single interview, it just means that there is another opportunity out there that is better suited to you and your future employer. It is not healthy to give in to assumptions and keep thinking about what could have possibly gone wrong because you can never know for sure. The only way is to continue moving and keep trying by applying to different places. What can truly help your future job applications is gaining the support of people who will advocate for you. These can be individuals you worked for part-time, on a project basis, or for an internship or a summer job. The third part of this chapter under 'Mastering the Art of Networking' will delve deeply into this topic. For now, I would like to introduce you to things you should look out for before, during, and after an interview so that you can attend well-prepared.

What to look out for in an interview

When you send your job application, your personality often doesn't shine through. This is precisely why interviews are extremely important; it is the best opportunity to show who you truly are. Granted, it might only be for a few minutes, but it is still a window for you to shine and stand out amongst the other candidates. I will focus on six key things to consider and look out for when you are entering the interview.

1. Are you your authentic self?

A lot of young applicants go into interviews trying to prove they are the best fit for a job title – as anyone would. Sometimes you might feel like you should act in a certain way to impress recruiters, you might start acting like someone else you look up to or you might introduce a lot of success stories to prove that you are capable. One important thing you need to remember is that when walking into that interview, you do not need to transform into someone else or start acting like you are extremely knowledgeable. All you must do is be yourself and be prepared to answer any question that will come your way.

One of the most important values that you can follow is that of honesty. During an interview, honesty shows that you can admit if you are unable to do something but are willing to learn quickly. This can be held in high regard by recruiters who are used to candidates twisting the truth to get their foot in the door. Some experts advise the young generation to say: "Yes I can do it" during the interview but only learn how to do something they are lacking once they get the job. I do not agree with this statement and would still prefer the truth over lying, and I'll tell you why. During your entire life, you are constantly gaining experience. There are multiple scenarios where hospitality qualities and skills are formed but we are not able to make the connection simply because it is not in the form of a traditional internship or job title. You could still showcase your skills and expertise by giving the recruiter examples that you can spot in your daily life. For example, you may be asked about your experience in leading an entire team, however, you may think, "oh I haven't worked in the hospitality industry before, so I don't have any experience in managing a team or working with colleagues in that scenario".

You don't always have to be in a set environment related to the job title you are applying for to be able to showcase your skills and experience. Being able to showcase your team leadership skills and potential could be done by simply sharing an example. Something as simple as being the captain of your university sports team could be used. The amount of hard work and dedication it takes to bring a diverse team together, make them feel like they belong, and create great synergy between all teammates to succeed during matches is something that can reflect well on your team leadership capabilities. We all know that being successful in different sport matches does not solely rely on a teammate's individual talent and capabilities. It is just as important for someone to bring everyone together so that they can work seamlessly and effortlessly. This is just one way through which you can show that you are able to create a strong connection within your team and help lead everyone towards becoming the winning team. Not everything needs to be linked to a specific work environment because sometimes we gain knowledge and talent outside of work and outside of the four walls of our classrooms. Even if this example does not relate to the typical on-the-job experience linked to the role you are applying for, it can positively reflect that you have the skillset that brings people together. Ultimately, it represents your potential to lead a team at work. We are constantly exposed to different events that help us gain experience, but our mind is used to compartmentalising our strengths by linking them to specific job roles. Our mind wanders down the thought process of, "Oh, well I never worked in that role before, so I don't have the experience". When we do that, we lose sight of the fact that this experience can be gained in multiple events, and it is not exclusive to one specific setting. That is why it is important to open your eyes to what is in front of you and be present enough to realise that you have a lot of experience. Becoming more self-aware about your actions and what you learn from every experience will help you gain confidence in your capabilities. Once you can do that, you will never feel the obligation to lie or feel less than when you walk into that important interview.

I want to share an example from my early career when I first started working at an international hotel chain. The year was 1996, and I remember this moment vividly in my mind. My colleagues and I were told to stand in a straight line as our supervisor came to ask us a couple of questions. The first question was, "Do you know what a cheeseburger is and how it is made?". We all agreed and said we knew, when realistically we did not know the answer. The plan was to learn afterwards, however, our supervisor proceeded to ask us individually to answer the question. When it was time for my colleague – who was also my friend – and I to answer, we couldn't. At that point, we were frozen and stuck since we did not know how to describe it in English and explain the process of making a cheeseburger. Our supervisor sent us home to memorise the process. We were only allowed to return to work once we mastered and understood the entire menu that was being served at the hotel. The main takeaway from this instance is that we really do need to be our authentic selves and we should not expect the worst outcome from our higher management. Being honest can surprise us in many ways. Initially, when we could not answer the supervisor's questions, we really believed that we would lose our jobs. That was not the case. We were pushed to learn and grow so that we could perform better at work.

So, here are three steps you can take which will bring you closer to your authentic self so that you can be yourself during an interview:

- **Research:**
  Before going for your interview, make sure you look at the different skill sets and responsibilities that are attached to the role you are applying for. This will be valuable once you arrive for your interview because you will be asked questions that surround those responsibilities. If you are not aware of these responsibilities and tasks, you will take a longer time to answer the questions which can make you stressed and nervous. And as you know,

we are not able to be 100 per cent authentic when our minds are stressed and racing.

- **Identify:**
  Once you have read the job description, create two different lists of examples that can help support the skills and responsibilities that are expected of you. The first list can include all the 'on-the-job' experience that you have gained, and the second list can comprise all the qualities you have gained outside the formal work environment. These are the examples that you need to keep at the forefront of your mind. Being able to identify both types of examples will not only help prepare you for the interview so that you can be your authentic self, but it will also make you less nervous since you know yourself very well.
- **Embrace:**
  Embrace the fact that you will never be 100 per cent prepared for an interview because you never know what new questions might pop up. Some recruiters may ask questions that you cannot anticipate or foresee. This is when your authenticity becomes more important than ever because you simply must be yourself and follow the answers that you think best represent your views and character. Treat every single job interview and the role you are applying for differently and as uniquely as possible. None of the two can ever be the same.

2. How can you show you are passionate?

It is very difficult to identify if someone is passionate when you are meeting them in person for the very first time. Just because someone is smiling and acting excited does not necessarily mean that they are passionate. Since interviews are short and many of them might only last on average ten minutes it makes it even harder to understand or judge someone's character. That is why some recruiters believe in asking the big question "where do you see yourself in five years?" to help them gauge how interested, dedicated, or passionate someone is about their career. I completely disagree with that approach because I find that it is extremely limiting. How can we expect someone in the stages of their early career to know exactly where they will be in five years? This question could harm the interviewee who might make up an answer on the spot and later after the interview continues thinking that they need to have a strong plan in place. This limits people from exploring their passion and what they are good at. One way of showcasing passion is by sharing a story throughout your life that reflects your passion for something that is related to the field or job you are applying for. It could be an example of a struggle you faced in your life and towards the end, you can turn it around into an amazing story. Storytelling naturally makes us want to relate to the other individual and understand them. Only examples or stories can showcase our qualities and the type of person we are. At the same time, you also need to be cautious of the time because if the interview is only ten minutes long, you would not want to spend half that time telling a story. It is also crucial to get straight to the point without adding unnecessary details.

3. What does your body language say?
Body language is a crucial aspect that can be overlooked by some when going to an interview. The way that we carry ourselves when we meet someone for the very first time impacts and determines the first impression we make. The smile, posture, the way the hands are shaken, and even the way you walk can affect that. When speaking and explaining yourself in an interview, you should ask yourself, "do my facial expressions communicate what I am speaking about?". If you are happy and excited about a specific question that is being asked, but your facial expressions do not reflect this, then the recruiter will notice. Sometimes short interviews can rely solely on body language and facial expressions because they can become the main indicators of whether someone is being genuine, honest, and themselves.

4. Be present
When you first enter the interview, try to observe what the atmosphere and environment is telling you. A lot of the time it is easy to lose yourself in your own thoughts and you start

preparing your answers before you are even asked. Of course, as you enter the interview room or when you jump on a video call, your main agenda is to present yourself as the best candidate for the role. However, during this process, you risk being too engulfed in your own thoughts to think about what is happening presently. When working in the hospitality industry you need excellent communication skills and great attention to detail. This requires the skill set of being present and it is highly noticeable when someone is present during a conversation. Being present can highlight your attention to detail, and level of emotional intelligence. It may seem surprising, but I can easily give you a couple of examples based on the interviews that I personally conducted where I tested the candidates' emotional intelligence based on their ability to read body language. It is important to see if someone is present and if they have a high level of emotional intelligence because they will be the staff who interact with guests daily. The way you talk and approach a guest is determined by their mood and how they are feeling. One way to understand what I mean by this is by thinking back to your own childhood. Remember those times when you wanted to go out with your friend but had to ask your parents for permission to go? If they were in a good mood you were more likely to feel comfortable to approach and ask them in a cheerful way. However, if they were in a bad mood then you would either wait for a later time during the day to ask them or you would change your approach. You might not have necessarily asked straight away, "Hey Mum, Dad, can I go out with my friend?", but instead you might ask them what's wrong or if there is anything you can do to help. The main point is that you would always approach them differently based on their current state and mood. The same concept is applied to hotel guests and that is exactly why it is important to find out if the candidate can be present enough to notice these signals that are being given by other people before they even speak. So how did I test their presence and emotional intelligence? I put on a sad face and looked disappointed at the start of the interview. I wanted to see who would notice and if anyone would step forward to ask. Out of all the people that I interviewed that day only two of them asked me if everything was alright and if something bad happened. Those are the two people that I hired. Out of everyone who applied, they were able to stand out because of their presence and their ability to pick up on my body language and facial expressions. Caring and creating beautiful memories for people are two important concepts within the hospitality industry. Now more than ever, emotional intelligence is central to everything that we do in our day-to-day lives. It is such a core pillar of the hospitality industry that we aim to bring smiles to everyone's faces when they stay at our hotel or when they decide to dine in.

5. Know the company you are applying for inside out

This is the most common and obvious point that I can mention, and yet, I still encounter individuals who do not properly know the job and the company they are applying for. Technology and phones are at our fingertips. We live in an age where every single person needs a phone to stay connected, so it is not difficult to do a quick google search to find out more about the type of hotel you are applying to. Doing this extra research shows the recruiter that you are interested in the company, and you want to work there. You can even go a step further by preparing questions to ask about the company or congratulating them on the latest awards or achievements if any of them were recently received. Curiosity and critical thinking can also be shown by mentioning that you have looked through the TripAdvisor reviews and can offer a solution to an issue someone mentioned. This can easily show the recruiter that you are forward-thinking and a team player because you are interested in solving a problem that is not even your own.

6. Be prepared to answer this question

The one question that is hard to answer but will give a recruiter great insight into the type of person you are is: "How do you want to impact people's lives?". This is usually the type of question that I ask people during interviews. I believe that we, as a society, can be doing so much more to contribute to helping others and everyone should be able to think of a way to do that. The person I'm interviewing might start discussing something they want to change; they could be sharing something they have experienced during their childhood that inspires them to help others. This person might not necessarily make a grand impact, but at least this question helps create awareness. In the end, our goal should be geared around how we can help people and it shows that the individual knows themselves very well and is in touch with who they are. When an impact is placed within the conversation, suddenly, the desire to make a lot of money or to get a promotion is out of the picture. It truly shines a light on what people want to achieve during their lifetime. It is a difficult question to answer but it is usually the people who care and want to have an impact on others who are usually the employees who work well in teams. This is because they start to look out for the entire team and not just themselves.

Ultimately, during an interview, you have the opportunity to stand out amongst the other candidates and truly show who you are beyond the words that are printed on paper. Every single individual is more than their high school or university diploma, and more than what a CV can truly reflect. Standing out is being able to show your passion through the examples and experiences you can share – the ones that truly moulded you as a person and impacted your mindset. Being able to share your vision of how you want to impact people is what distinguishes you from merely being given a title. Everyone wants to grow in their career, however, by showing your vision you can reflect that you are more than just a shiny title placed on a pedestal. This is what makes a person different, having that purpose of how they want to make a change, and being able to distinguish the specific challenges in the industry and how they can provide solutions. Sometimes you may know the challenges an industry faces but you may not have the solutions just yet. Solely being able to acknowledge the challenges and creating awareness around finding solutions showcases a curious and innovative mindset. These two aspects are intrinsic to how a leader operates and assesses what the industry needs. In the end, if you do not pass the interview stage, it is always important to reach out to the management team to find out how you can further improve or understand why you were not able to pass on to the next stage. This can help you learn, and it serves as a growth experience. I would like to introduce you to some personal examples related to the different times that I held interviews and what I have noticed when interviewing prospective candidates. I believe that this will help you see things from the interviewer's point of view, and it will also make you more self-aware about the way you act when you are in an interview. There are five main things that I want to highlight:

1. Your facial expressions

When I meet candidates for the first time, the first thing that stands out for me is always the smile. You can always tell if a smile is genuine or if it is fake. Some people smile only with their lips, but a true smile extends to the creases created by the eyes and the face in general. This is the first thing I look for because our mind is used to picking up these signals and we subconsciously create preconceived ideas about someone based on such signals without even noticing them. If someone is not genuine when you first meet them, this will affect their interactions with guests at the hotel.

2. Curiosity to learn and keep in touch

There were a couple of cases where the interviewees were not hired and did not pass on to the next stage. What really made them stand out during the interview was the fact that toward the end they asked me, "What is one best practice that I can learn from you?". They were asking me to mentor and guide them by answering some questions so they can still benefit even if they were not hired on the spot. Some of them also wanted to keep in touch and asked if they were able to reach out to me in the future if they had any questions related to the industry. This does not happen very often, and it's these types of genuine personalities that stand out and encourage good networking and connection.

3. Personalities with high emotional intelligence

During interviews, I like to ask individuals to share their personal experiences and examples of times when they have made a difference either in the workplace or during an internship. The way they share their story and start their story is directly related to the type of person they are. As soon as they start talking only about themselves and they do not mention other people within the story, it shows that they are very self-centred. Being able to speak about other individuals, how they felt in a specific instance and how everyone interacted with one another reflects that someone is aware of the present moment and has the emotional intelligence to gauge how people feel.

4. Quick responses and taking action

However, if someone is self-centred, it becomes even more apparent when the story is extremely long and dodges the final point they are trying to convey. Adding more and more information does not necessarily mean you are adding more value. Sometimes saying less has a greater value because you are getting straight to the point while saving time. When you are under a limited time constraint, being able to communicate efficiently is beneficial. If stories are too long and very self-centred within an interview, I usually have to jump in and change the conversation to the next topic, otherwise, we will not have enough time to get through all the questions. The way this type of trait reflects within a workplace is in the form of tasks or decisions that are being delayed or dragged on because conversations are too long. A lot of the times when we sit in the boardroom to host a meeting, a lot of conversations take place, but we are not able to come to an agreement or course of action fast enough.

5. Identifying efficient problem-solvers

The reason I sometimes ask someone to share a story of a time in their life when they faced a huge challenge or problem is to check their efficiency in problem-solving. Someone who spends more time talking about the problem and repeating the same points, rather than focusing on how the obstacle will be overcome, is usually someone who takes too long to implement the solutions. In some cases, this causes a lot of negativities in the workplace and a toxic environment for other employees that are part of the same team. Personally, I would like to hire someone with a go-getter attitude and positive mindset over someone who will continuously complain about something that they can work to change.

These are the main five things that you can look out for when you step into an interview in the future. Becoming more self-aware about the type of signals you send with your body language and the way you answer questions can change the way you are perceived.

Keep your eyes wide open – every life event offers a new lesson

I am often asked by students who are pursuing degrees in the hospitality industry about how fast they can become managers in a hotel. This question highlights one of the main challenges that we are still currently facing within the hospitality industry – a generation that easily leaps from job to job, in search of quick results and promotions.

As I read multiple articles and keep up with the news in the hospitality industry, I came across various interesting findings. Currently, it is believed that millennials were the most "impatient generation" in the workplace. Most of them want to progress rapidly in their career. So, when millennials and the younger generation ask us, industry experts, how long it will take them to become a manager or become successful in their career, I have three main thoughts to share:

1. **There is no success formula** – before becoming a successful manager, you need to understand yourself and your purpose within the hospitality industry. Being able to identify why and how you want to impact peoples' lives, because, after all, you are entering an industry that adopts a people-centric approach, where people are at the heart of all operations.

2. **Understanding everyone around you** – a managerial role is merely a title, and the most important part is the change that the person behind this title brings. It all starts with understanding all the cultures and the people that surround you. To get to a managerial level, you need to build the right emotional intelligence and empathy towards the people that your hotel will ultimately serve. This takes time, practice, and patience.
3. **Gain experience through hard work** – the knowledge and theory that is learned at university need to be complemented by hands-on experiences. It is not enough to learn from textbooks, as the main lessons lie within the daily interactions you have with people from different backgrounds.

The two main skills that you can only learn through experience – which does take time – are those of connecting with people and building patience. Usually, you are advised to enrol in an internship program or a traineeship during the summer, which is extremely important, but it requires you to be heavily invested. This can only happen during the summer holidays, but what about throughout the year? I believe that we can learn how to improve our human connection and build patience through jobs that are completely unrelated to the hospitality industry.

For example, you can apply for part-time promoter opportunities, and this will teach you how to react and respond to different types of people based on their background and their current mood. In the hospitality industry, you meet different kinds of people, and not everyone is in the best mood all the time, so this opportunity teaches you how to better interact with individuals through practice.

Secondly, you could apply for a part-time call centre job. The multiple phone calls during the day can help you understand what it takes to become persuasive, patient, and calm. In the end, no matter how bad the previous call was, you need to reset and pull on a smile and happy tone for the next person you are about to call.

These two jobs are merely two ways through which you can build habits that last and gain a better understanding of how to converse with people with humility, understanding, and patience. The next topic that will be discussed is the way you can create a strong network, whether through interviews, meeting people, or on-the-job.

Mastering the art of networking

When applying to different jobs, networking and the ability to build a strong professional relationship can help you gain stronger reliability since you have an army of individuals who believe in you and advocate for you. In this world, we can never achieve things all on our own, we need to depend on others who have been in the industry for a longer time to truthfully vouch for us. This becomes extremely important during an interview where you are only able to get to know someone over the span of ten minutes. Having this additional layer of support in your toolbox will help you stand out in the competitive pool who may not have the same recommendations as you. There are two ways to network, one way includes tactics that are outside of your daily work environment, and the other set of tactics are found when you are immersed in your day-to-day workspace.

Networking outside of the work environment

The following ways you can network combine tactics that can be applied by students who are currently still studying and individuals who are looking to build connections that are no longer studying. Here are a couple of places and methods through which you can initiate the beginning of a professional connection.

1. Conferences

Whenever you have the opportunity to attend panel discussions at a conference or summit, you can make the most of the event not only by gaining more knowledge from the speakers but also by interacting with the different people who are present. Everyone that attends a conference is brought together by their common interest in that specific topic. By attending these events, you are already automatically filtering out the people who are not related to your industry or area of interest.

You can stand out during these conferences by sitting in the front row and engaging with the speakers when they open the floor to the audience to ask any questions. Being present and actively listening to the discussions taking place will help you come up with challenging questions. These are usually the type of questions that will attract everyone's attention since it might be something they did not think of, or it might be something they also relate to. After the panel discussion is over, some people might approach you to further discuss your perspective because they find your views interesting.

If people do not approach you, then you can approach them to start conversations, especially if other individuals introduced questions that attracted your attention. Being able to identify the people you resonate with will ensure you can pursue meaningful connections with people who have similar values to you. Everyone has their own agenda and purpose when attending these events, and at times they might not have the time to interact, however, if you create a memorable impression, they might make time to connect.

Complimenting the organiser of the event is also another way to show interest and connect. You can approach them to compliment and congratulate them on creating a successful event. Building a good relationship with organisers can open the door to meeting other individuals that are in your industry, and you can also offer them your support in the next upcoming event. This way, you both benefit from this exchange of services. When you adopt a mindset to add value and support others, you will always be able to spot opportunities that you can be part of.

2. LinkedIn

Once you have attended conferences you can easily add individuals you have interacted with or personalities that you may have wanted to talk to but did not get the chance due to time constraints. Sending a personalised message on the day of the event referencing the conversation you had will make them more likely to remember you and accept your request. Posting about the event, what you have learned, and your own perspectives can turn into useful insights not only for your followers but your new connections. This way you can start engaging and connecting with people on a deeper level.

Another way you can build connections on LinkedIn is by commenting and engaging with other people's posts. Building trust and forming a connection with a person goes beyond just exchanging emails or sending that connect invitation on LinkedIn and then never meeting again. It does require a lot of effort, but the true connections will flourish the more time you dedicate to them.

3. Tapping into existing networks

The number one supporter you already have when you are at college or university is your professor. They all have multiple connections and they have already built a vast network within the industry since they have been part of it for a longer time. You can easily tap into that network by reaching out to your professor and asking them to introduce to you different experts or lookout for any specific opportunities that you want to pursue. Not only will your professor be ecstatic about you taking the extra initiative outside of the classroom, but they will also be happy to help make a difference in your life. Tapping into existing networks can also be achieved by becoming part of Facebook or WhatsApp groups of like-minded individuals who are looking for the same opportunities and are also sharing them with the rest of the members. You never know who can introduce you to someone and at the same time, other members can also benefit from your connections within the industry.

Technology is valuable because it can quickly connect people and you can find out about opportunities without having to be present at a specific event if you are unable to attend. This gives you the flexibility to find out more in a more efficient time frame.

4. Guest speakers at universities

Universities have a vast pool of connections and through the academic year, they often bring various guest speakers to shed light on specific topics. The best part of these events is that they are free of charge and all you need to do is show up to be part of it. These networking opportunities are served on a platter and the way to stand out is by showing interest and asking questions. When a guest speaker presents at a university it is usually an unpaid event for them and they are going out of their way to share knowledge. Whenever a student is eager to learn or when they ask questions, the speaker will feel excited and happy to make a difference. This is why engagement is the highest form of standing out, especially since some students might be too shy to ask anything. During one of the universities talks I presented, I promised to mentor the top five students who asked the most interesting questions. Not every speaker will offer to mentor students, however, it does not hurt to ask them yourself after the event is over. They might agree to it and that way you can learn from the best and tap into their networking circle. You might even be able to offer your support and secure an internship in the future through them.

5. Volunteering
Applying to government-run and company-based volunteering initiatives may prove to be un-paid at times, however, it adds a high level of experience. There is always something to learn from supporting the execution of these events and it opens the door to meet individuals who can open other doors for you. Certifications and recognitions showcasing your high level of engagement can be added to your portfolio to strengthen it when you apply in the future. Every experience offers a different lesson.

These are five of the things that you can do to build strong connections when you are in college or university, but what about the relationships that you can build while at work?

The secret of building a network while working

Being part of an internship program, working as an entry-level or, being a trainee in a specific company exposes you to multiple networking opportunities that might surprise you. Networking helps you attract people that will later in the future advocate for you when it is time to apply for another job or when you are working towards turning your internship into a full-time position. The first step to gaining support and trust is the secret ingredient of building a strong relationship and gaining support. Being traditional and going with the flow is easy, but if you want to stand out, you need to take one step further, and that starts with being able to manage your emotions. Working in a new place can be tough and challenging, and if you let emotions control you, then you lose focus on the goals you are trying to achieve. It is important to push away any negativity that you may encounter in your daily tasks and focus on how you can change the environment to turn it into a positive one. Passionate individuals are always the ones who stand out and become memorable. They are the ones who later become role models for their entire team. At the end, when you want to apply for a full-time position or you want to move to another workplace, you will be remembered. So how do you achieve this? Here are five methods that can help you stand out and become memorable to build strong connections within the work environment.

1. Making the first move
Sometimes waiting for the right 'season' when job applications are open to send your CV or cover letter might prove to be too long of a wait. So why not make the first move? You

would approach one of your already established connections or someone in an industry that you would like to be part of and simply tell them: "I would really love to help this company and be part of it. Give me the chance to prove myself over the course of two to four weeks. I will work for free and if by the end of this trial you believe I am the right fit for this team and the position, then we could transform this into a full-time position". Not a lot of people take the initiative to offer their services and solutions to a company. This is a unique way of grabbing a recruiter or manager's attention. There is nothing to lose and so much to gain if they agree to let you work on a trial basis.

2. Adopting the right mindset
What is classified as the right mindset? After all, that statement sounds subjective. What I mean when I say adopting the right mindset when working I am referring to thinking and acting as you have already secured that full-time job. By thinking you have already transitioned from your trial or internship period to a full-time permanent position, you start to adopt a mindset that is looking to help colleagues and different departments because, in the end, you are looking out for everyone's interest. When you start doing that, the people you work with will slowly start sensing your enthusiasm, excitement, and

willingness to go above and beyond. This will help you create good connections within the workplace, and it also leads me onto my next point which focuses on gaining support from colleagues.

3. Gaining support from colleagues

Go the extra mile by being there for them when they really need it, whether this is to cover an extra shift if they are unavailable or have an emergency, or perhaps offering support when they need it. We all like feeling supported and knowing that someone is there for us. Doing that and not expecting anything in return will help you gain the trust of your colleagues. They will not only trust you, but they will also feel like they can depend on you if they need to pass on a task. Your colleagues will soon appreciate the hard work and extra effort you are offering. When the time comes for a peer review or assessment, they are going to be the ones who advocate for you and the ones who will speak positively since you were a team player and we're able to offer support. In the end, you are not being helpful to gain something or achieve a hidden agenda. Being helpful and supportive should naturally come from within, and sometimes support is just a by-product of that. People will naturally support and help one another when they receive the same type of treatment.

4. Keep asking questions

The best way to improve and grow on the job is by consistently asking for feedback or tips for improvement. Remember, silly questions do not exist. Colleagues and managers will appreciate the initiative and they will start seeing more and more potential in you. Interacting with other departments, getting to know the people and asking them questions will also expose you to new information. The ability to understand how all colleagues work and how everything co-exists in a work environment will help you see the bigger picture. Asking questions and showing interest will help you build good relations at work.

5. A reliable reputation

Interns are usually remembered for one of the two reasons: they were exceptionally helpful and that is the type of person that someone would want to count on for anything, or they messed up extremely badly and they will most likely not be considered for a full-time position in the future. How do you want to be remembered? Usually, you can do ten great things, but it takes one mistake to taint that reputation. Building that reliable reputation is dependent on your involvement, participation, and willingness to volunteer for every opportunity that is open to everyone. When you take more initiative, not to simply show off but because you genuinely want to help people around you, then you will be recognised as someone reliable. It is important to try as many different tasks as possible and job positions when interning to understand what you like and what you are good at. Everyone is talented in a specific area and following that path will help you become an expert in that area.

Gaining support and building connections that will advocate for you is not just based on gaining experience, but it is based on a person's attitude, skillset, curious mindset, and ability to remain memorable. Becoming memorable all boils down to the type of person you are and how you can make everyone's job easier by working as part of the team. All you need to do is make sure that you are giving your 100 per cent. There will be ups and downs because you're entering a completely new environment, with new people, different nationalities, and there are a lot of different things to learn. Some people may only do the bare minimum but that is where you need to take charge and exceed everyone's expectations. All the examples that were shared above encapsulate a person's positive mindset and willingness to help others. Once you can do that, you will be able to build a strong network of connections. I will next discuss recruiters and how leaders can keep inspiring their colleagues to create a healthy work environment that helps everyone grow.

CHAPTER 5 INTRODUCTION

Often during the recruitment process, multiple recruiters get caught up in searching to find the 'right' candidate who ticks off a huge list of requirements. This can range from having specific skillsets, a university degree and various job experiences. Throughout this process, the type of character and personality of the candidate is overlooked at times. I believe that recruiting individuals who have high emotional intelligence, empathy and compassion are at times more valuable. A degree does not necessarily mean that someone is automatically more fit for a position. I personally found that passionate, enthusiastic, and authentic individuals who have a high emotional intelligence grow and accelerate much faster in their roles. It is not always easy to identify or test someone's emotional intelligence or passion for a job. However, that is exactly what I will be unveiling within this chapter.

5

REINVENTING THE RECRUITING WHEEL

Someone can have a perfect education and resume but might not be the right fit for the company. This chapter will explore the importance of fostering a company culture that not only attracts individuals who show tremendous potential but one that creates a supportive environment for its employees. Before jumping into that aspect of company culture, it is also important to figure out how to search and filter the right candidate for the job. One that can easily fit into the work culture and has common values. This chapter is mainly geared at recruiters and higher management as it helps them identify specific characteristics of individuals that can help them understand the type of person the interviewee is. Overall, being able to pinpoint the type of person someone is helps determine whether they are a right fit for the company culture. In the previous chapter, there was a heavier focus on the candidate that was applying for a job. It is important to place the magnifying glass on the other side of the coin and focus on how the recruiting process can evolve to become more efficient.

From my years of professional experience, I have found that the individuals who learn quickly, accelerate in their career faster than their peers and positively impact their work environment are the ones who possess skills that are related to two main qualities. These qualities are passion and authenticity. So, what do I mean by those?

Passion

Passion is enthusiasm and love that is expressed towards something specific. In this case, when I speak about passion, I mainly refer to being passionate about living life to the fullest and having a positive impact on the people that surround us. An individual can only embrace their passion for living life to their fullest potential when they understand who they are at their core, what values they hold and what purpose they want to follow during their lifetime. Sometimes people may not have it all figured out, and that's fine because our perspectives are constantly changing, and we always follow new ideas and thoughts. The most important thing is maintaining the daily positivity and drive to chase our dreams and vision no matter what life throws us. In the hospitality industry, being passionate about human connection, communication and interaction are extremely important. We always remember how people make us feel during interactions and everyone can sense someone's attitude towards them. Individuals who are passionate about pursuing a specific purpose will do everything in their power to make it work. They will ask questions and have an unstoppable drive to gain knowledge so that they can grow in that direction. This is precisely why someone passionate about entering the hospitality industry will not only learn quickly but also progress at a faster rate than others.

Authenticity

Individuals who prove to be authentic do not try to be like someone else. This means that they are comfortable in their own skin and proud of the type of person they are. Competition and ego are pushed to the side, and they do not feel threatened by their colleagues. In this respect, they are usually the individuals who want to bring everyone together to work seamlessly in a team. They are also the type of people who want to help others shine and see them succeed along with them because they do not feel threatened by others' talents. The authenticity also helps them embrace honesty in their capabilities, experience and what they can achieve. Authenticity helps someone understand themselves and keep them grounded and humble.

But often, we see that the current hiring process is standardised everywhere. Before taking into consideration authenticity and passion, this process relies heavily on the following:

1. Having a university diploma or degree
2. Make sure you have the certain experience to join as an entry-level employee
3. Being able to provide recommendations from past employers

These are the first three areas that are looked at and the main disadvantage in following this process is the risk of eliminating multiple talented individuals who are passionate and prove to be authentic. Individuals who did not have the opportunity to afford tertiary education are excluded from being able to prove themselves and show that they can thrive in a specific job. These individuals may have not necessarily come from a rich family, but they could possess an unshakeable drive to learn and ultimately excel in their new role. Some people do not have a diploma simply because could not afford it. They have very little experience but that does not mean they should be left alone. As leaders, we need to look at this situation in a different way by putting ourselves in their shoes, by understanding that we are all human. Of course, we all need to feed our families and survive, but you can also see it in peoples' eyes when they want to make a difference and when they badly want to be part of something bigger. So, we must take this opportunity and bring them on board because the drive to contribute and make a difference shows in the way people complete their work in the long run. This is precisely why I believe that we should move in the direction where we can change the mindset that recruiting departments adopt when hiring new talents in the hospitality industry. Instead of following a standard template, why not post a recruitment advertisement or post stating that any talent is welcome if they can show why they are fit for a certain job. This is where the different life examples come in and neatly tie in with what recruiters look for. This provides a way for both the recruiter and applicant to explore whether this role would be the right fit for the candidate, and they can both honestly decide together.

We all need to shift from the mindset that work experience is only gained through a university diploma and through already working in a similar role that someone is recruiting for. A lot of the time when we look for 'experience', we miss out on potential candidates who are high performing individuals eager to evolve and learn. Now, you could argue and tell me, "But Rikhsibay, most of the hotelier industry experts look to hire the best candidates because there is a certain image to maintain and strict standards. How can we change this?". We know that not a lot of people allow someone who is not highly experienced if there is someone better than them. It is seen as extremely time-consuming to train someone from scratch and it can take a while for them to get used to everything. A lot of people are afraid of this risk mainly because of lack of time, taking a risk on someone who might change their mind about continuing to work with you once they are trained, and because they do not want to risk the image of a brand in case the new trainee makes mistakes. So how can these perspectives be changed for the better? It first starts with understanding the importance of making time for this proper training and onboarding once the right candidates are selected for the specific roles. In this fast-paced world that is constantly focused on results and the greatest level of output, slowing down to offer the right type of support can improve the quality and efficiency in the long run as colleagues are better prepared.

Another aspect that I would like to highlight is the requirement of a diploma is a necessity on a recruiter's checklist. Four to five years of study is most sought after, as well as an additional masters. Sometimes we don't really look at how much experience is gained in the field itself, interacting with people and coming up with solutions for day-to-day challenges. The main differentiator of hiring someone who has a diploma over someone who has a significant amount of experience from on-the-job interactions is pure ego. Some individuals who graduate with a bachelor and master's degree feel like they are entitled to reach a managerial position as soon as they graduate, however, they do not possess the understanding of ongoing issues and problems that the workforce faces. At times, they are also the type of individuals in a work environment who would not be willing to do a job that is below their job description simply because they believe they are superior. The mindset of "I did not study for such a long time to do this small job. This is not my responsibility, someone else should do it". The problem with this approach is that these people become 'bosses' who try to be master puppets in a work environment, and they look out for themselves. This does not contribute to cultivating a culture of understanding, happiness, and care. It can also be linked to an authoritarian style of management that can drive employees away from introducing important conversations as they fear being fired. That is just one depiction of the multiple scenarios that we can encounter.

Going back to the initial point, the main perspective that recruiters need to adopt when hiring is to hire promising individuals – regardless of educational background – if they are able to showcase that they are passionate, authentic, have a high level of emotional intelligence, and are driven to grow in their role. When speaking about passion, emotional intelligence and being able to understand someone's nature, we can all agree that is it difficult to do so during a short interview. First impressions are important, but they are not necessarily the ultimate representation of someone. So how can recruiters identify these qualities?

Firstly, being able to identify emotional intelligence in another person is only possible if the recruiter understands what it means. Emotional intelligence is the ability to understand, manage and handle not only our own emotions but also others'.

Knowing yourself

Knowing yourself is the first step towards achieving great emotional intelligence. What I mean by that is being able to truly understand the feelings behind who you are: your own likes, dislikes, passion, purpose and what you want to achieve in life. Understanding the feelings and motivation behind these aspects helps you know yourself. Sometimes old, negative habits take over our lives and these have been instilled in our being since we were young because of past experiences. However, through reflection and understanding, we can help heal those parts. Once we can recognise those old negative habits, we can work toward changing them. Ultimately, the more we understand ourselves, the more we can understand others without becoming defensive or feeling attacked if a certain chain of events occurs before us. This is one reason why emotional intelligence is very important because if you understand yourself, you will get to work on yourself. And no matter what happens, no one can stop you from pursuing your vision or goals because any negative feedback or criticism is either embraced for the better to grow or if it is inaccurate, you can deflect it since you know who you really are. It will take time to master this, however, if you don't, then you will not be able to manage and control your feelings and reactions in different scenarios. Often at work, I am sure you can sometimes see that the people are not happy with what they are doing, right? They force themselves to follow a career path that they do not enjoy and a job title that does not make them happy purely out of necessity or because they are chasing the money. I remember speaking to a 35-year-old, and I asked him, why are you pursuing this position if you are unhappy with being here and following this direction? This showed me that people are fully capable of planning their misery by staying in a job that they do not enjoy just to save up and retire. Their main goal is making money and then laying back to enjoy the last part of their life, however, this can be avoided if you understand yourself, know what your purpose is and once you figure out how you want to impact the world and the people within it. Every single individual has the key to unlocking their own happiness. No one will ever appear out of nowhere to make you happier and satisfied with yourself. This feeling of happiness, acceptance and understanding can only be accomplished by you. The temporary applause of others when you achieve something great is not enough to keep you happy and you will constantly chase the next big thing to keep that satisfaction going. If you are unable to make decisions that fulfil your own heart and decisions that will create a positive contribution to the world, then you will have multiple fluctuations in moods. Sometimes you are ecstatic and sometimes out of nowhere you become sad. You must keep working to find out the formula that works for you that will ultimately help you understand yourself and your future vision: one that goes beyond chasing recognition or fame from parents, teachers, peers, or anyone else. There is nothing wrong with changing your career path or the way you live life if you are not happy. If you like something then you go for it, but you need to become an expert in that field if you believe that it is your calling. Of course, this does not happen overnight, and it will take a few years, just like any self-development path. Following your passion and leaving a workplace or situation you are unhappy with is a hard decision, but you have nothing to lose and a great load of happiness to gain.

Adaptable

Someone who is highly emotionally intelligent can easily adapt to a new environment and respond accordingly. It is easy for that person to do so because they can understand someone else since they can place themselves in their shoes. This introduces a plethora of benefits in a working environment because it can easily solve conflicts, help others feel better and overall create a healthier work environment in which everyone works together rather than against each other. When you can understand someone's emotions and the reason behind why something happened, you do not give into reactive emotions of anger or mistrust which stem from misunderstanding. I want to share what emotional intelligence looks like through two personal examples of mine because I believe that we can understand concepts a lot better when we are given real-life examples.

The first example showcases empathy, building connections and high emotional intelligence. A part of this also involves being able to read body language which I will also break down step-by-step after introducing you to the example. I was first exposed to these aspects when I was young. By now you already know that I used to get involved in so many different business ventures and I spent a lot of time with older individuals trying to learn from them by seeking answers to the million questions that were running through my head. So naturally, instead of playing football with the neighbourhood children or any friends from school, I would often spend time listening and talking to older people who had experience. After school, I would always find five to six elderly people sitting and having tea together. You might think that they are just the old people who would sit outside their front porch talking or gossiping about everyone in the village. I can assure you that it was not the case at all! I would often sit and listen to them. One thing that I noticed every single time is that there was always two or three of them that would lead the conversation. Talking, sharing, and telling stories of their past. During that time, everybody would patiently listen to that person and curiously waiting for the story to end. It was usually these top three individuals who would, in a way, control the crowd and guide the course of the conversation. When I was young, I did not know anything about controlling the crowd, but now I can see that they were the ones who would guide the conversation in different areas. Sometimes they would also give me advice and I also started to ask them questions.

That was one of the first times that I witnessed empathy and later realised that it is achieved by being present with the people around you and truly listening to what they have to say. When one person was talking, everybody was paying attention. Once everyone would leave, I would continue to sit with the main person who would always talk and share their stories. I wanted to be able to talk to them alone and get more answers. I noticed that even when we sat together, every single person that crossed the road would say Salaam Alaikum (greetings) to that person. These older people who are well-known in your town, are the ones who are respected because they care enough to listen and always help.

I noticed that every town had this older person, almost like a tribe leader, who connected everyone emotionally by bringing them together to have these enlightening conversations. Whatever the tribe-like leader would say, people would trust. Before, I did not understand that listening, giving advice and being helpful to everyone helps you not only earn respect but also introduces you to more opportunities to support the community. But when I look back at that moment, I can understand why everyone knows this person, how he knows everyone's story, how this person is emotionally connected to everyone and why so many people respect him. It all started with him inviting anyone to have tea with him and introducing conversations. There were only a few people who understood the need and necessity to connect with people and the power of active listening. Once he started to listen to people's stories, understood them and offered his advice, more and more people started to go visit him. Every village has that one intellectual old person that everyone goes to for wisdom because they are 100 per cent emotionally connected. When people show this level of interest and understanding with no judgement, a safe place is created where ideas, problems and concerns are voiced. Advice is then given, and the solutions make people happy because they trust that it will work when applied.

Now imagine this tactic was used presently in a working environment. If all the employees would be able to go to their manager, supervisor, or their team leader to comfortably share their story or the specific area that they need help in. Wouldn't that environment create greater happiness for the employees because they know they have someone they can count on for advice and support? You can spot a leader with high emotional intelligence by looking at the people who are part of their team and whether they are open enough to approach their leader to ask any question. All of that is part of emotional connection. As the years passed, this experience helped me realise that at the end of the day, no matter what you do, where you go around the world and what you see, it is our responsibility to take care of different people that cross our path. This is something we need to keep in my mind because it is not only about the money and the promotion. Now that I have shared the example, I want to further explain the importance of emotional intelligence in the workplace.

Importance of emotional intelligence in the workplace

In the hospitality industry, everyone is constantly interacting and conversing with one another, whether it is colleagues, guests, or business partners. Once people understand and know themselves, they can better interact and converse with others. So, the next time they enter a room and more than ten people are sitting in the area, they know exactly how to approach and interact with that person. This is because they can read their body language and understand whether they are in a good mood or a bad mood. Based on how the other person is feeling, you adapt to that environment accordingly and manage the situation differently. We are also able to react differently when given feedback or criticism if we have high emotional intelligence. Sometimes people find it difficult to interact with clients or guests that are in an angry, irritable, or aggravated mood. So, if the employee does not have high emotional intelligence, then they can feel threatened and their confidence also plummets when criticism is thrown their way.

Their reaction to the situation could also not be controlled or managed properly which can create a greater mess. This leaves the guests with a bad impression and ultimately reflects badly on the hotel and brand as a whole. People remember how you make them feel and the bad experiences are always remembered by anyone who is visiting a place on vacation because they expect everything to run smoothly. At the end of the day, we spend a lot of time judging people, we spend a lot of time thinking if this is right or wrong. But you don't know every single person's back story and what happens behind the scenes. This is especially true when people go on social media saying negative things. Even if a person is a rising star, if they do not have high emotional intelligence, they can easily get affected if they receive a negative comment on social media. They will automatically think, "Oh no! What will I do, shall I delete it, what should I say?". This is where the disruption happens, and if you don't direct yourself properly, you will see it as a threat as well and it will push you in a downward spiral. It is important to be able to know how to take the pressure, whether it is from parents, friends, neighbours, taxi drivers, and anyone that crosses your path. Life will be beautiful if you can handle external pressures because you can manage your emotions and reactions.

Now after explaining what emotional intelligence is, and why it is important, I want to share how it can be identified during an interview. After all, this chapter is about reinventing the recruitment wheel. I could not dive straight into the recruitment process without explaining what I mean by emotional intelligence within the context of hospitality. I can identify someone's level of emotional intelligence by asking them certain questions and observing how they respond and react if they were placed in those scenarios. So here are the **three** questions that you can also use to gain insight into someone's emotional intelligence, passion, and the type of personality they have. Always remember that being able to analyse the reaction and responses is only possible if you have a deep understanding of your own emotions and if you have a high level of emotional intelligence yourself.

Question number one: What is one that you have done that changed somebody's life or made them feel completely different?

Through this question, I want to find out if this potential candidate has been involved in decision-making processes or part of bigger projects that had a positive impact on others. This is not a process to identify if the person is good or bad because that is not the goal or scope of this question. People are people, and everyone has a different way of thinking or reacting towards events in their lives. My focus and attention are geared towards understanding whether what they are saying is genuine and if it is flowing directly from their heart or not. I analyse that by looking at the following aspects:

1. Their smile – what is it saying?

You can always tell if someone is speaking genuinely by paying attention to their body language. Are they looking at you with a smile on their face? It cannot be any type of smile because it is also easy to tell if someone is genuinely smiling or just faking it to come across as passionate or interested when they are not actually interested. Someone is smiling genuinely when you can see creases at both ends of their eyes, their cheeks are rising higher and both corners of their mouth create creases. Have you even come across someone who was only smiling using their lips and mouth? When the eyes do not have creases at the ends, that is usually when it is a fake smile, and it is easy to recognise that. So, you will be able to tell if it is a real smile by paying close attention to their facial expressions and their eyes.

2. What is the storytelling approach?

Another aspect to look out for when they are answering is how much they relate the story to themselves and if they can put themselves in someone else's shoes. If they truly changed someone's life or made them feel different, are they able to identify how the person was feeling before their help? It is important to find out whether the candidate can start speaking about the other individual first rather than placing themselves at the centre of the story because the story revolves around how the other individual was helped. When the centre of attention is placed around the significance of them helping rather than the person who was helped, then you know that the conversation is power-driven rather than support-driven. The message that is being introduced out there revolved around the narrative of, "I did this, and it is because of me that this happened. If I was not there, then it would not be possible". I am interested in the way that the story is told overall. This is when the candidate's true character and personality are reflected. The story is going to be portrayed in a couple of ways, but you must see if the story is very egocentric, right? There is a difference between making the story all about themselves and whether they are genuinely talking in a way that exudes pride and a genuine feeling of truly wanting to help. This helps to distinguish whether someone did something for a specific person because it was in their heart or if it was done purely to gain fame or recognition for their own benefit. I always look for a person who wants to help without a hidden underlying agenda because those are the individuals who can place their ego aside and not give in to it. A huge ego can result in unhealthy and toxic competitive behaviours.

Question number two: What solution did you come up with that made a difference?

When asking this question, it is similarly important to observe once again what the body language is telling you. By looking at their eyes, you can tell whether they are really talking from their heart. Through my experience, I find that the more genuine and truthful someone is, the more eye contact they make. They can focus on the story without looking around the room and constantly changing the topic. When someone is talking about a solution that they came up with to make a difference, it shows that they involve themselves in the decision-making process regardless of whether they are required to or not. It shows a willingness to go above and beyond to come up with something new that has never been done before. At the same time, it also shows that they have an open mind to try things differently because sometimes we do not find a solution during the first try and it might take multiple tries to get there. This willingness to not give up and try reflects how someone can be determined, and consistent. Coming up with solutions naturally highlights how someone is not afraid to make decisions and mistakes since every trial of finding a solution comes with the price of making a mistake or the risk of failing. It is the decision to try and find a solution despite the fear of mistakes and failure that helps distinguish a true leader. Finding solutions comes hand-in-hand with taking responsibility and if anything does go wrong, it is the ability to stand up in admitting that it did not go. This shows that the person tried their best regardless of whether they knew it would succeed or not. At times it is hard to find people who would go out of their way to take responsibility and protect their team for the solutions that they all came up with. Being a leader and becoming a team player means protecting others who are part of the process. The answer to this question can also tell you is someone worked on their own to find a solution to an issue because no one else was willing to support them or if they were able to convince people to support and bring them together. Each of these scenarios shows that the individual has persistence, great communication skills and a bright mind. The example that they are sharing does not matter, what matters is how they achieved coming up with a new solution and how they were able to contribute to the team in the end.

3. Make them feel comfortable

Sometimes people have the answers to the questions that are being asked within an interview, however, they could still get anxious and nervous about the situation. As leaders, if we notice that they are getting nervous, we should help them feel more relaxed and comfortable about speaking their truth. One way to break the ice and make things easier for them is by sharing an example of something similar you went through. By changing the subject, the attention is taken off them and suddenly you (the interviewer) become the person that is being interviewed and they feel like they are the ones who are interviewing. Once put yourself in their shoes and create a matching mirror image, you can begin to understand how they feel. As you start latching onto that feeling you can then think of a moment in your past that you also felt that way. Maybe you can give them an example of a time you were nervous at an interview or in any other situation. By doing so, you are normalising that what they are feeling is completely normal and it is not something to be ashamed about. Some candidates research a lot about how they should behave and act during an interview, but this can make them feel overwhelmed when the time comes to interact with an interviewer. A perfect scenario is etched into their mind, and they try so hard to fulfil that to the point that it paralyses their speech. I know you know what I am talking about because we have all been there at some point. We try so hard to show our best qualities that we forget to be ourselves. This is why it is so important to start relating to them and to gain their trust so that they start talking the way they normally do, and they feel more comfortable being themselves. After a certain level of comfort is achieved, I then take control of the conversation again to bring it back to the initial question that I asked. This time I pose the question in a different way to see if they can answer. This is when you will be able to get an authentic answer from them that is not scripted to perfection and where they feel comfortable with themselves. If the person is still nervous at the end of the day and you are unable to make them feel comfortable, you will understand if that job is for them or not. They will be able to tell you immediately if they are passionate about it or if they were just applying for the sake of getting a job.

4. Figure out how important the job is to them
If someone is coming to a job interview and they are trying to shift their career from one area of the hospitality sector to another, you need to find out why they decided to do so. It might have to do with wanting to feel greater satisfaction or they realised their passion lies in another department, but they need to be able to answer why they have made this change. Being able to answer this question shows where their interest and where passion lies. The next follow-up question is asking them what they have done since the day that they decided to switch their career path. Maybe they decided to switch six months ago. If there is anything that they have done to work on themselves so that they can prepare themselves for this move. This can be anything from seeking training part-time somewhere, getting advice from somebody who is an expert in the field, reading a book on the topic, or even watching education videos online to

gain further information. There is plenty of free information on YouTube and various websites. If the candidate has not done anything since they decided to make this move, then it signals that they are not that interested in the job, and it is not that important to them. They have obviously not done any research or done their homework about the industry. I would be willing to give someone an opportunity if they really show the potential, they are highly interested in making the switch, and are self-motivated enough to reach out for information without someone telling them to. But if they are not, then this is when I am straightforward with them and I tell them, "Look, you might not have this opportunity here with us, but you might go somewhere else after three or six months for an interview and this kind of question may come up again. But you must be ready next time. So that means being able to tell them about the type of industry and job you're applying for.

5. Always give someone hope at the end of an interview
It is not possible to accept every single person that attends an interview. At the end of the day, only one person will be selected for that specific role and there will be people who will need to walk away and accept that. Sometimes it is better to help make that process easier for people by helping them learn something during the interview. This will make them

walk out the door with more knowledge than when they first entered. Additionally, it is also important to help boost morale because leaving an interview with rejection can demotivate people especially since we never know how many times they have been turned away from a role that they really wanted. So here are three things that you can do to help boost someone's confidence, help them gain more knowledge, and introduce them to new insights.

Offering feedback

Often interviewees do not hear back from recruiters, and they do not find out why they were not selected. This can be extremely frustrating because when you are on the lookout for a job, you always want to know what factors contributed to not being selected. Being able to narrow down whether it was linked to experience, skillset or personality can be helpful to any applicant as it gives them direction for areas of future improvement. Some individuals do not even receive the news that they were not selected. This is the equivalent of being 'ghosted' by the corporate world. This is why being able to receive feedback on why someone was not chosen can help give direction for the future areas of development.

Giving advice

Once you know that the candidate will not make it through to the next round and you know that you will not be selecting them for the next step, you should be able to offer them advice. This will help build their morale and they will feel less confused and lost about the reasoning behind what they see as a rejection. By giving them advice on how they can further develop to be equipped for that role, you can hopefully shift their perspective into a positive one. It can be difficult to keep going forward without any direction or feedback. When someone receives advice, they can level up, rather than applying for the same roles and being denied the position because they still do not meet certain requirements. Additionally, you can tell them to try again in six months or a year once they have applied the advice and filled the gap. This mindset helps them become positive and pushes them to excel because they know there is still potential for the future. They may not come back and apply at the same place, or they might already find something in the meantime, but at least you were able to help them gain that momentum. In the end, you have also had to create a lasting impression on them that you truly do believe in them. This speaks volumes because not all recruiters take their time to give feedback on the spot and take the time to explain things.

Maintaining connection

Regardless of whether you decide to accept their application or not, you can let them know that you will always be in touch with them if they ever need advice. This assures them that they are not alone in the application process, and they can always reach out to get further advice, feedback and mentorship that can help them when applying for a new position or securing another interview. You must learn how to build that connection and support with all the people that you encounter because you never know the impact you can have on them. You need to feed the person positivity and inspiration as they leave the interview. Give people hope after an interview even if they did not get it. You can tell them that they didn't get it but help them see the silver lining. Once you have given them advice and feedback you ensure that they are not left helpless. This also introduces the prospect of them returning in the future and coming back again after some experience.

This is mainly what is missing during the process of recruiting someone. The way that the industry needs to change is heavily linked to emotional intelligence, body language and how people react. When someone has a strong willingness to learn and can admit that they still have a lot to learn, then you know that they have a humble personality. It is a lot easier to teach someone who embodies a positive attitude towards their role and someone who is actively engaging with their team to come up with new solutions that can benefit everyone. Their ability to manage their emotions is extremely important because it dictates the ease with which they can integrate within the new team dynamic. Now, more than ever, with multiple cities increasing their diversity across the world, the ability to understand other cultures, people, traditions, and perspectives is extremely important in maintaining a healthy and inclusive work environment. People with low emotional intelligence find it hard to relate to others and cannot understand them easily. Within a workplace, especially like the hospitality sector, which is a melting pot of tourists from all over the world, it can be detrimental to the day-to-day tasks where they engage with all sorts of nationalities. All these details may seem simple and easy to follow, however, not everyone can pick up on the small signals. Once the candidates are selected to be part of the team, the advice, feedback, and growth disappear. If anything, it becomes even more crucial to ensure the development of the onboard new employees. Their success, the way that they are trained, how they grow over time and whether they feel supported, determines how they progress in their career. This is what we call developing future leaders since ultimately leaders will not be in those positions forever and they need to properly train the people who are just starting to take over when the time is right. Which brings me to my next chapter, how can we develop future leaders?

CHAPTER 6 INTRODUCTION

The future leaders are now walking and living amongst us, and they are ultimately the ones who will come up with new ideas and ways to make the world we live in a better place. This is a time when they look for support, and guidance so that they can learn their vocation just like we did once upon a time. Mentoring, providing free online sources, and nurturing current workforces are three areas of development that I will be speaking about in-depth. This chapter is for successful leaders and individuals who wish to share their wisdom, knowledge, and experience to help enrich our current youth and employees.

6

DEVELOPING FUTURE LEADERS

Having already spoken about new recruitment processes, what to look out for in candidates and how to identify certain desirable characteristics that individuals may possess, it only makes sense to discuss how to support the further development of the team that has formed. The points that I am about to share with you do not only apply to candidates who have already been offered jobs after the interview process or the ones that are already part of the hospitality workforce. The advice and discussions offered are also inclusive of the youth who are still studying and anyone who possesses the interest and drive to seek further education not limited to afford the cost of an educational degree from an institute. Future leaders and people who have the potential to make a difference are hidden across the globe. This chapter covers topics related to mentoring, creating greater access to education, and delving into the crucial elements needed to cultivate a supportive work environment.

Let's talk about mentoring first. I want to split this into three different parts, mentoring for students, the workplace and anyone interested in learning no matter their background, profession, or experience level. This way, no one is left out and everyone can have access to information without barriers that prevent them from gaining it. These barriers could be in terms of not having access to the right network that can direct you to a proper mentor who is willing to share their experience, or it could also be related to not being able to afford education.

Mentorship for students

Being able to mentor students and support them on their journey of becoming the leaders of tomorrow is a privilege anyone would be lucky to undertake. It is a huge responsibility but a rewarding one at the end of the day. For me, taking this step forward was extremely important and necessary. Growing up, I had to always ask people and really put myself out there to learn from others' experiences. I was not mentored or taught by anyone at an early age. That is exactly why I want to offer my knowledge to the younger generation, the young students who are determined and excited to learn from someone who has been through it already.

Towards the end of 2021, I created a mentoring program for five eager students. I picked these students at the end of a guest lecture that I conducted at their college. At the very beginning of the session, I told them that I mainly wanted to interact with them, answer their questions and have engaging conversations, rather than just throw too much information at them. I even told them that the top five students who come up with the most interesting questions will be chosen to be part of my first mentorship program for a year. It was great to see surprise and excitement painted all over their faces during the announcement. You could easily see how their eyes lit up with eagerness and how they were already starting to think about what question they would like to ask. Taking this step to approach universities and students requires experts and leaders to step out of their comfort zone. As a leader, you do not have to wait for a university, professor, or institute to reach out to you because they might not. So, why not be the one to take the first step forward to offer your expertise as a guest speaker at the university? Based on that, you can see if students would be interested in a mentorship or trainee program.

With all the knowledge that leaders have compiled over the years, there is so much to share and so much for students to learn from us all. We all need to start becoming leaders who volunteer to interact with students. In the end, these students are the future leaders who will be making the big decisions. These mentorship and trainee programs should be free of charge for the students, and they should not pay to apply or take part. The main benefit of this is students gain access to learning experiences without having to worry about spending extra money and being able to rely on the mentor for advice and life-changing decisions.

I do not believe in the concept of hogging knowledge and information. During all these professional years and the different roles I have undertaken, I have realised that each one of us has a different story and experience to share. So why keep all those unique stories and learnings to ourselves? A lot of lessons are learned on the job and getting insight before experiencing those situations first-hand could either help a student avoid making the same mistakes or prepare them for those situations so students know how to better react. There are multiple scenarios where mentoring can fill the gaps of knowledge that the university does not offer. Mentors can offer unique advice based on their career progression over the years and share their expertise when it comes to making life-changing decisions. There are plenty of benefits of mentoring the youth and I could continue to go on about it, however, I want you to hear it straight from the five students that I am currently mentoring. They will be sharing why they wanted to be part of the mentorship program and why they believe the sessions we hold outside the classroom are completely different from the ones they have in class. Here is what they think:

Anika Ahmed

During the guest lecture, I asked, "How do I stay motivated despite any setbacks or negative experiences, such as incidents of mass firing during the pandemic?". This was the question that helped me get selected to be part of the mentoring program. When I first heard Mr Rikshibay speaking, I felt inspired to be mentored by him. Although he holds a high position in a reputable hotel chain, he did not hesitate to talk about his personal struggles and humble beginnings of his career. It was the elements of honesty and openness that made me take an immediate liking and trust towards him. During his talks, he emphasised the importance of kindness and personal gestures of gratitude towards all employees, which I also believe in. Lastly, since I am in Dubai for the first time and do not know anyone, I thought it would be helpful to have the guidance of an experienced local in the industry. During our first online group meeting, I was honestly not expecting much out of it, but I was amazed to see how Mr Rikshibay was utilising his break during work hours to help us. In this industry, free time can be so limited and precious. The session was very productive. I left feeling more confident in myself and my doubts were cleared. He answered many questions we had and really boosted our self-esteem for our future careers and when job hunting. Although our faculty provides us with the standard guidance and support, having mentorship from someone currently holding a high managerial position in the industry can make all the difference. He gave us insights, tips and tricks for behaviour and conduct at work. This also included insights into how we can improve certain skills that are not being taught at school. The mentorship comes with exposure and more networking opportunities, which really gives my profile a boost that I would not get otherwise. He talks about the outlook on life, career, relations but more importantly how to stay motivated.

Awad Alawan

My main question was if you could succeed in the hospitality industry without being humble. The reason I want to be part of this mentorship program is because I believe that there is no better opportunity to learn other than being with someone with this much experience and exposure to the industry. At first I thought it was only going to be regarding school but after the meeting with Mr Rikhsibay, I discovered that it's more of a personal program. The difference between the mentorship program and university classes is the lack of school involvement. This gives us the freedom to express ourselves without having to accommodate any rules or regulations.

Alina Dzebisova

The question that I asked was: what advice can you give us, as freshers, to achieve the same success as you have? I wanted to be part of the mentoring program mainly because of my passion for the industry and my potential. With the right guidance and support, I am sure that I will make a great contribution to this amazing industry. Mr Rikhsibay provides the right support, guidance and is able to share his valuable experience. This is all-important for us as young students. The mentorship program has given me an opportunity to broaden my horizon and knowledge. It truly made me aware of my strengths and the specific areas of improvement that I needed to work on. I believe that both, the University program, and the mentorships are extremely important to obtain the necessary knowledge. While classes provide us with more theoretical approaches, mentorships are able to introduce us to the practical aspects from the point of view of operational professionals. This helps us understand things better.

Miriam Ferrulli

A classroom, students and a speaker. During the guest lecture held by Mr Rikhsibay, we were talking about his professional career, how it started and the pathway he followed. It was not smooth and started quite soon because as a young child he had to take the initiative to take care of his family. I was emotionally immersed in every word of the story and I was deeply moved by what was being shared. I felt as if I was living it. At the end of the speech, I asked if it was possible to deliver such strong emotions within the workplace and make others experience this as well. I will always keep his story in mind during any hard times of growth as an example of achieved success. Being part of the mentorship program means a lot to me because it gives me the opportunity to be guided in the right direction and it helps me choose the best pathway to become a successful leader. My first impression of the mentorship program has been positive. Our first video call as a group was exciting and the program Mr Rikhy created for us made me feel lucky to be part of it. The mentorship sessions differ from classes because I feel supported as an individual, and not just a student that is part of a group. Although I am not alone during the sessions, Mr Rikhy is capable of making everyone feel seen and heard in the same measure.

Yash Patil

When I asked Mr Rikhsibay "What is your dream?", he told me that his biggest dream is to donate most of his earnings to charity. I think this question was more of a winning question for me personally because it showed me that humanity is still alive. The reason I wanted to be picked for the mentorship program by Mr Rikhsibay is mainly because when he told us about his tough journey and how he worked hard to get to where he presently is, it really proved to be a great motivational experience. So, I thought that working with a man who has built his own empire without having any support from anyone would be great for me. Not only to become more motivated but also to have a second dad in Dubai. Our university focuses more on education, which also important, but I personally think that experience plays a very important role in our journeys towards success. Mr Rikhsibay shares his experience and education which makes the sessions different from university.

This is what five of the students from HTMi Switzerland Institute in Dubai, who are part of the mentoring program, had to say about their early and fresh experience so far. Esther Lawrence, the learning and development manager at HTMi Switzerland Institute in Dubai also shared her thoughts on the importance of mentorship:

Esther Lawrence

If you are like me, you probably studied, had a career in mind and chose a career based on what your parents told you. Alternatively, you might have chosen a career based on the grades you got, or the college or university options that were available at the time. You started your career, and it may or may not have been what you expected. You were not prepared for the career world, or the field you chose. What seemed to be exciting as you studied, the dreams you had of all the money you could make, and the car you would buy, were then drastically shattered when you realised that you had no idea what being an accountant, a lawyer or a hotelier truly is. You merely had an idea with no real insights into the career you chose, but you eventually figured it out as you grew. However, had you gotten some guidance or had the opportunity to learn from someone in the industry maybe you may have had a better glimpse of what you wanted to do. This is exactly why there is a need for mentors today more than ever. It is crucial to coach and guide the younger generation towards the career path they have chosen to pursue. To enrich their minds with the possibilities of the path they chose and offer guidance as they progress. This is a call to all professionals and experts that enjoy their work, to step up and become the inspirational force for the new generation. I believe that mentoring is a gift that keeps on giving as it opens students to developing their leadership, improves their relationship-building skills and creating a more meaningful network.

Some of you might be wondering how you start mentoring. It is extremely simple, and it all begins with taking the first step in reaching out to schools and offering to talk during different sessions. Your guidance and advice can provide insights to students to help them eventually secure an entry-level role. This can done through one-on-one sessions or as a group setting. With the digital age making a huge sweep across the globe, connecting has been made even easier with virtual meetings. I am sure we can all agree that we all could use guidance in our careers and majority of us have come across a leader that has truly inspired us, helped us develop and has given us direction to get to where we are today.

In the same light, I believe that everyone has something unique and special that someone else could benefit from and learn from. There is no better way to teach than to be a mentor to a young mind. In the words of Tim Minchin in his speech 'Nine Life Lessons' at the University of Western Australia, he says: "Be a teacher, even if you are not a teacher, share your ideas, don't take education for granted, rejoice in what you learn and spread it". We all have something to offer and more than ever, we need to start sharing with everyone.

As an educator, I have seen the positive impact mentorship has on a student's progression and growth because they were exposed to a greater in-depth understanding of the industry and field they are pursuing. A strong connection between the mentor and the mentee is created, and that enables them to appreciate the world of work to better navigate through the choices they have to make. This will help them avoid bursting their own bubble as everyone has to start somewhere.

Inspiration is drawn from multiple people and new leaders are nurtured with the right guidance. These same leaders will then grow to become mentors to others as they truly understood the power of mentorship when they were taken under someone's wing. I do hope that more and more experts heed the call to become mentors.

That was Esther Lawrence's perspective on the importance of mentorship and there are plenty of other experts out there who agree with this initiative too. I know that a lot of experts and individuals want to share their knowledge with others. However, I often hear that the main barrier to mentoring students is the inability to find time throughout the day. Multiple people get wrapped up in their hectic and busy life and they start to believe that there is not enough time to do it all. I do not agree or believe this. Personally, I believe that if an expert wants to mentor someone, they will always find a way to make time and adhere to this commitment. Of course, it is not an easy task because it does require 100 per cent commitment to assist, develop, and help them grow. They really do have a lot of questions; their mind is filled with curiosity, and they want to see the work differently. At the same time, they are also fast learners because they are passionate and have gone out of their way to be part of the program. This type of drive shows that they are there to learn and truly develop themselves because no one pushed them to be part of something they were not interested in. This is also a good way to filter out future potential employees and leaders because they will graduate in a few years.

The way I look at mentoring is similar to how a person interacts with a baby. When we take care of a baby or spend time with them, we look at what they are doing and where.

But during that time, your entire focus and attention are 100 per cent focused on the baby. Whether it is playing with a ball, following them around, helping them stand up to walk or creating a playful puppet show for them. You look at the baby and the baby will look back at you, a powerful two-way connection is created. It could be for one or two hours. That is how I look at mentoring, when I mentor, I truly become present in the moment through active listening, interacting, and giving my undivided attention. I forget everything else, and my focus is only placed in the mentoring sessions during the time that we all meet. It is important to identify the different directions they all individually need support in and then how they can get that support. Most of the time, I sit and listen to what they have to say and the more we meet, the greater the emotional connection. Mentoring is not just picking up the phone, jumping on a call and merely asking who they are and what their career plan is. Building future leaders takes time and it happens gradually. Students need constant support, advice, and someone with experience to lean on.

So how do I make time for mentoring? Well, I usually make time for it during my day off. I allocate half a day or a full day solely for mentoring. When I conduct Zoom calls, it is after work between six to seven o'clock at night. The reason I always have the time is that I make time for it. Ever since I committed to contributing to helping shape the youth and being there to offer guidance, I made it part of my life routine to be there. This is why I believe that when someone says they do not have the time, it is just an excuse. Most of the people have two days off, and there is always room to place one or two hours aside for students. My advice to leaders is to stay positive and jump out of the mindset that there is no time. If you can place discipline as a core action driver, structure the way you operate during your day-to-day to achieve a good life and work balance, then I am sure you can always find time to mentor someone. It does not have to be a large group; it may only be two to three different students or graduates who are eager to learn. Usually, with a large group, you are unable to see huge results over time and it is better with a smaller group of, at most, five people. That way you can follow a structure where two individual goals must be achieved by each student by a specific time. Then the personalised feedback can be given to each one of them and tailored to their unique needs. Since I never had a mentor and I had to figure things out on my own, I realised the importance and power that mentorship can have on others. This is true not just for students but also for employees of all levels because learning and improving never ceases. Next, I want to introduce why it is important to continue mentoring and guiding individuals within the workplace and how you can create an environment where they feel like they can reach out for support.

Guidance and mentorship within the workplace

When people stop their career growth, they feel like they have remained stagnant for a long period, they start looking for new environments that can take them to the next level. These thoughts could be slowly simmering in their minds for months on end until finally, it reaches a boil, and they decide to leave. Management at times would be shocked and they may see this as a decision that has come 'out of the blue'. However, I believe that the signs are all around us and they are multiplying day by day. We all need to be present and willing to look out for them. At the same time, if guidance and mentorship are offered daily, then employees are less likely to leave from lack of growth. Here are some ways a leader can guide, mentor, and continue keeping staff members motivated.

1. Consistency

Providing mentorship, feedback and guidance is an ongoing process. Having individual meetings once or twice a year to evaluate someone's progress and set new goals for next year is not as effective. The consistency of checking in on staff members and understanding the daily struggles they face will help them evolve and grow a lot quicker. When a leader checks in with their team daily it also shows everyone that they are cared for and listened to. This is another way through which they feel supported. This is why it is important to be present with them during on-ground operations rather than giving everyone the same feedback during long meetings.

2. Explaining

Make sure that everyone understands their roles and what they need to master to either be given extra responsibilities or become eligible for a promotion. Everyone has a different level of understanding and, as a leader, sometimes you need to step up and start explaining things differently. At times, a big goal might sound difficult or daunting for individuals. To make things easier, the big goal can be cut into small little pieces so that the big picture is not intimidating. When basic goals and tasks are introduced, it is easier to understand the bigger picture, and this makes it simpler for everyone.

3. Recognition

Like the advice, feedback should be given consistently, providing recognition for something that has proven to be extraordinary is extremely important. This is especially true when trying to maintain morale, happiness, and motivation within the workplace. When any colleague is working extremely hard, going above and beyond their mere job description, coming up with an innovative solution to current problems that teams are facing or they get a positive review from guests, that should be recognised immediately. This on-the-spot recognition is extremely important because it shows that you are paying attention, you appreciate their efforts, and other colleagues will also be able to celebrate this achievement. There is no point in waiting until the end of the month or year to recognise only a few select individuals. By that point, no one will remember the instance and it feels outdated. It can also feel like it is a forced or mandatory initiative by the human resources department because it is the end of the year or quarter, and they need to show support. Creating consistency with recognition and appreciation as soon as it happens also brings the team together because they are not competing against one another for those limited slots for awards. Colleagues start to engage with one another, and they also begin to show consistent support since anyone can be shown appreciation as soon as they stand out and work hard. Having two or three awards at the end of the month creates competition that can pit people against each other since they are all aiming to achieve the glory that comes along with the title. Additionally, since these awards and recognitions cannot be made public every day since everyone gathering can disrupt the workflow, a WhatsApp group can be created. This way, in addition to the leader going to tell the colleague personally of the great job they've accomplished and why they can also post on the group with everyone. Pictures, certificates of appreciation and positive feedback can be shared with the group. Over time, people start to recognise that they are not competing with one another over these awards, and they start to engage together; people start to support one another. It is important to pay attention to how the supportive message is being delivered and communicated. You can also introduce the team to new goals that they want to learn or achieve. Not only does this create equality in terms of attention, but it also makes people feel like they are appreciated, heard, and seen. Leaders should never look too busy or too important to listen to people.

Mentoring employees does require consistency, understanding, patience, and the ability to make time to show you genuinely appreciate and care about everyone. This is what makes the difference in work environments where most people feel like everyone is too busy to acknowledge their contribution. Supporting and talking to your team is what motivates them to do better and to constantly work towards improving over time. I also believe that mentoring, advice, and feedback should be a resource that is available to everyone, not just students and individuals who are already within the workplace. It should not be a luxury or benefit that people are exposed to only if they are lucky enough to be in a work environment where leaders are willing to nurture them or if they are financially stable enough to gain access from an academic setting. I strongly believe that anyone interested in improving their skill set in a certain direction should have access to the support to do so. Free access to a bank of information or knowledge can solve this and it can easily be created merely by experts sharing their stories. I would call this an online mentor's academy!

Online mentor's academy

Technology is more advanced than ever before, we are undergoing the fourth industrial revolution, and the perfect platform can exist. Imagine having this online bank of knowledge that is compiled of different stories, experiences and advice that stems from senior experts in the hospitality industry. An online platform that shares knowledge with everyone free of charge. A group of us, hospitality experts, can start this and once we decide to do so, we can all hold each other accountable to follow through. I want to bring experts together so that we can all share our knowledge. The way I see this platform, if we are looking at the bigger picture, is as a bank of ideas, stories, and knowledge from different countries across the world. This way, even someone in the village can learn even if they cannot afford to study at an institute. The final goal is to reach everyone and educate people for free, to give multiple people the idea that they need to contribute day-to-day. It could be used by someone in the village, who is taking care of a cow or two, but has the internet and is eager to learn. They will know that ultimately there is life after cows, and just because you were born into a farmer family does not mean you cannot change and take a different path. We are stuck in a system where knowledge and information are reserved for the privileged and no one wants to break this system. Fewer people will invest in educational systems if they cannot be monetised.

Another strong pillar that contributes to developing future leaders is ensuring that employees are happy in their current position. For this to happen, everyone needs to feel comfortable in their ability to approach their management, and they need to feel secure in their job. Three ways to achieve this are by creating security, supporting individuals emotionally, and being able to create a strong connection with them. Here is how you can achieve that:

Creating a strong connection with employees

Listen to your employees and work hard to understand their point of view without jumping in to tell them that they are wrong. Being able to understand employees, their struggles and why are acting a certain way can not only give you an insight into the reasoning behind their performance at work, but it can also open the conversation into figuring out a solution if something is not going right. In the end, we are all human and we want to feel like we are part of a tribe. When we know that we are part of a place that cares about us, wants to listen to us and ultimately wants to help us become better, then we are more likely to go to work with a smile on our faces. Being in a happy and positive mood pushes people to work happily and they do a better job in the long run. They start to realise that they are part of a team that is supportive rather than out to compete with everyone. This makes it less stressful because they also start to look for opportunities to help others around them because they were uplifted. Having at least two or three people who can make you feel like you are not alone really does make things easier, and it is sometimes even inspiring. This domino effect creates an environment where everyone is looking to help one another and it forms a true team, or as I like to call it, a tribe. What I like to see is colleagues popping up like a mushroom, out of nowhere, to surprise their other colleagues with support and help when they need it. In the end, we all need to come together as a team and look out for one another.

So, you might be asking yourself, "What does happiness have to do with developing at work"? Well, I have seen people thrive and grow a lot faster in a work environment where they felt supported, heard, and understood. If you are miserable, constantly looking to see how much time you have left until you can go back home for the day and if you are subtly passive-aggressive with your colleagues, then are you are not enjoying working in that space. This type of scenario will ultimately push people to start looking for another job where they feel like the entire team wants them to succeed rather than fail. Building a strong connection with colleagues requires the trust to be able to speak about certain things. This can only happen if there is enough trust and if you are someone who gives the impression of being approachable. These are the next two points that I want to discuss.

Building an approachable environment

I always believe that true leaders are the ones who can first hear what their peers, colleagues and staff members have to say before they even start to speak. The individuals who speak first and make everything about themselves, are usually the ones who are not emotionally connected to their team. It is usually in those scenarios that empathy and emotional intelligence is required most. An example that I look up to is that of Nelson Mandela's father, who was a chief and tribe leader. Every time his father used to take him to the tribe discussion when he was young, there were two things that he noticed and learned from him. The first was that everyone sat in a circle facing one another and the second was that his father would speak last. Someone else would start the meeting, and everyone would speak. This way everyone thinks, "Tribe leader is listening to us, tribe leader cares about our issues and cares about our emotions". In the end, the tribe leader will not correct anybody and tell them that what they said was wrong. He would ask further questions so that the answers could build the conversation and only at the very end, would he introduce a small speech to end the meeting. But real life dictates the opposite. You will mainly see someone who is supposed to be a leader, but they are just a boss or part of management because they always speak first. Only a small percentage of higher management can truly be called leaders and adopt the approach of encouraging colleagues to speak first before they do. My vision is for everyone to create an approachable environment where people know they can introduce their concerns, new ideas, solutions, and feedback without being rejected. It is important to create a culture that embraces ideas from all levels and roles within the company because you never know where a brilliant idea might be hiding. Micro-management creates barriers between people, and it is a robotic style from an emotional intelligence perspective. People do not feel connected when someone is constantly watching their every move, ready to comment on the mistakes. Under a robotic and autocratic management style, individuals cannot perform their best and they will be forcing themselves to be someone they are not. Passion and happiness will not exist in a workplace where creativity and brilliant ideas are squashed. Understandably, sometimes people are still not comfortable approaching higher management with ideas because of the stigma that has been introduced into society. People may still hold fear of losing their job if they were to approach someone in a higher position with fresh ideas or there might be a slight fear of rejection. There should still be an option to share feedback and ideas for the individuals who feel that way. Creating a board of employees or union that is made up of the team leaders of specific departments could be a way to solve this barrier. The team leaders do not necessarily have to be part of HR or the managers of that specific department. These team leaders could be selected based on how they get along with the people in their team, whether they are the most approachable amongst their peers and they could even be selected by their own team members. Introducing this democratic approach shows that there is a way to have everyone's voices and ideas heard. Through this board of employees, more feedback can be brought to light and any issues can be resolved. Bringing people together like this can increase their confidence since they are being supported and heard. It can also additionally improve their speech and the way they pitch their new ideas. Overall, the more people interact, engage, and work together as a collective, with all their interests pooled in together, the closer the team becomes. It shows people that they are all on the same page, working together to improve their joint environment rather than feeling like they are competing against one another. This helps build greater connection, trust, and unity.

Nurturing our internal talent first!

Often, it may seem like an easy option to bring someone on board from outside the company, someone who has multiple degrees and may have a shiny resume filled with different experiences. However, they are not the ones who are familiar with the work environment and culture of the place. So, why not prepare for it with your internal team and start setting up career growth conversations with them. This way you can understand what direction they want for the future and what position they are striving towards. A common reason why individuals switch jobs is if they feel like they are stuck at the same level in their career, no matter how hard they work to reach new heights. I like to believe that we are all lifelong learners who will never truly reach a point where we know everything. This is precisely why career development talks can help introduce the steps individuals need to take and the methods needed to reach their desired level. Supporting your internal tribe to rise to higher positions will motivate them to work towards achieving those requirements and can ultimately mould them into a better fit for the position than someone hired externally.

Encouraging creative thinking

I often hear, "Oh look, that hotel is doing this, let's also do that", or "Look they are becoming popular, and people are visiting them because of that, let's also introduce that here!". Being inspired by other people and what other companies are doing is great as long as it does not dim our own creative light. The only way to stand out in this industry is by doing things differently, otherwise, we become part of a system that copy-pastes everything. So, can we stop using examples of how others are achieving things and start following our own ideas? This is when listening to colleagues and team members become so crucial. Listening is not only beneficial in terms of making people feel connected, but it also introduces an abundance of ideas that remain locked away if not encouraged and cheered on. My mother would similarly cheer me on with every single business venture idea I had when I was only fourteen years old, I have learned to applaud every single idea that colleagues would share. This creates room to discuss and debate to see how we can implement new ideas and through conversation, we can all decide if it is something worth pursuing. Applauding ideas encourages people to think of new ways to contribute and it does not push them away or make them think, "Oh that was a silly idea, I won't ever share what I think because it is embarrassing when they reject me". This is why it is important to focus on how you can bring your team together to find new solutions and ideas, rather than searching to copy what the competition is doing. Rather than just pointing fingers at others, we should stop comparing because every single person and company has a different destiny and path.

Supporting people by being there for them

Creating an environment where people are not afraid to be themselves is pivotal to ensuring that people are comfortable enough to introduce a conversation about any issues they are facing. It is easy to have all the resources and support in place for whoever needs it, however, if the individuals do not feel comfortable enough to approach someone, then it does not make a difference. Eliminating the rigid procedures and the mentality that no mistakes can ever be made instils fear and stress in a working environment. A culture that embraces learning from mistakes and not repeating them proves to be healthier for all. You do not need to give them a functioning manual or book of how they need to act or behave. At our core, we are all emotional human beings who want to be able to express ourselves. Otherwise, we become robotic and follow a mundane program and task list without going the extra mile to try new solutions. Creating an environment where you are approachable goes together with establishing trust, understanding and openness. Leaders should also ask for feedback from their staff members so that they also know how they could improve. That can further build trust and it helps them evolve. Here is an example that encapsulates how I created a safe environment for someone to b open about sharing their problems:

One day I was just passing through my workplace and I found myself in the elevator with one of the staff members. He happened to look at me and asked if I had eaten and we both found out that neither of us had. I was not able to talk to him further that day because I was in a rush but I told him to pass by my office the next day so we could speak more. Our day continued and the next day I found myself with the same person and he asked me the same thing again. This time I paid more attention and asked him why he didn't eat. His English was half good and half bad, but we were able to communicate well. So, I asked him why he was not eating. He mentioned that he is fasting on Monday and Tuesday. I was surprised and asked him why he was fasting. He then decided to tell me that the main reason was that his father is drinking a lot and fighting with his family. The family back home in his country were not well off and his mother and sister were suffering a lot there. His sister was deeply unhappy and cried daily. This was why he decided that he would pray to God and fast because then hopefully they would be in a better situation. Initially, he did not want to talk to anyone about this because he believed that no one really cared. I assured him that I cared and that I wanted to know more about how he was doing. That's what pushed him to open the conversation and tell me that his sister will be getting married in January. He hoped that things will be better then. I told him that when the time came for her to get married, I would personally contribute to the wedding and help him out a little. Since I have six sisters, I understood how stressful and hard it was to carry the entire family by supporting them. I knew exactly the type of pressure he was facing so I wanted to help relieve some of it. His face lit up and he automatically changed his mood. The fact that someone was there to listen to him, and he felt supported made a difference in his day. When I saw him the next day, his attitude was completely different, and he was smiling. So, this is emotional intelligence, feeling, reading, and understanding body language. If I did not ask this question, he might not have told me what was happening in his life. But deep inside his heart, he felt that he should communicate with me in the elevator. So, that meant he wanted to build the conversation. This is just one of the many current examples that I have when it comes to supporting people at work beyond things that are related to work. Since we have focused a lot on the present state of the hospitality industry, I would now like to examine the future.

CHAPTER 7 INTRODUCTION

There are multiple areas of growth that I would like to speak about where I would be able to offer some of my ideas and solutions. This book does not encapsulate everything that I want to express, and it will be the first of many. The one thing that I want to focus on here is how we can make the hospitality industry more inclusive for everyone. More specifically, looking at people with special needs and how their hotel stays will be memorable and stress-free. I have a couple of solutions that I have not seen being implemented. This is one way through which I plan on opening the conversation on this topic, and if you resonate with my vision, then I would love to hear from you.

7

THE FUTURE OF HOSPITALITY

During every single step of my life's journey, every moment, whether it was related to my personal life or my professional career, I always relied on the values I learned from my family. The values that originally emerged from Uzbekistan's culture and traditions. Now, no matter what challenges or questions arise, I can rely on and fall back on those values. This is precisely how I look at the future, and now more than ever, this is especially crucial since we are all excitedly looking ahead of time. When it comes to the hospitality industry, there is always room to evolve and become more flexible, adaptable, and inclusive. One main concept that I believe will truly tie everything together stems from my cultural upbringing and the experiences I was exposed to. One value that I learned and carried with me to this day is from a wedding celebration that took place back home. The value encompasses equality and sharing. You may wonder, "How does a wedding celebration even relate to the hospitality and hotelier industry? They are two completely different things!". Bear with me, you will soon understand the importance of these emerging values. Now we all know and expect that just like all other international weddings, multiple invitations are usually sent out to all the family members, friends and loved ones. Then, on the big day, all the guests unite to celebrate this unique and cheerful moment that brings together two wonderful individuals. Seems straightforward, right? Well, the way we celebrated was unlike any other typical wedding because it truly adopted an 'open-door' policy. This meant that anyone from anywhere could join the celebration without having to present an official invitation. Every single individual that passed by could join, and no one would ask "Who are you?", "What are you doing here", or "Why are you even here?". The feeling of isolation and privilege was taken out of the equation. Multiple people pooled in to join the celebration that day, with more than 700 people that included neighbours from different streets, their friends, and even strangers who happened to pass by. Everyone felt welcome to join and there was no awkward feeling that they did not belong there. As the day went on, you could slowly see the dust rising in the air as everyone started to rejoice and dance together in the open garden of the house. A lot of the people did not know each other but everyone was having a fantastic time and they were enjoying themselves. During this wedding, there was no differentiation between very important people, rich or poor – everyone's title and status did not matter because they were brought together by one main and common purpose – celebration. Even people who would not normally be able to afford to watch live performances would finally be able to attend the wedding. The air was filled with happiness from all the clapping, singing, and dancing. During the present day, it is easy and simple to differentiate between people based on their class, earnings, and work status. It can be seen through the different seating areas on planes: people either sit in the economy, business or first class. The wedding taught me the true meaning of acceptance and equality. It made me realise that everyone in the world deserves an equal opportunity regardless of their background, status, gender, and upbringing. By this point, you might have a couple of ideas about where I am heading with this thought process. It is all about offering individuals equal opportunity and a healthy environment within the hospitality and hotelier industry. There are two sides to this coin: one is about building a healthy work environment for all the colleagues, and the other is about offering guests equal opportunities. Building a healthy work environment has a knock-on effect on the way co-workers complete their daily responsibilities and tasks. It breeds a positive and happy workspace where employees are more likely to offer guests a great experience because they will be happier and more attentive. Being in the hospitality industry for more than two decades has taught me how to create an amicable working environment where the entire team thrives and works together rather than adopting a competitive mindset. This formula is based on four core principles:

1. Approachability

As a leader of any team, you need to be approachable. This means that every single team member can trust you and feel comfortable approaching you at any given moment in time without feeling scared or ashamed to do so. This not only creates a stronger team dynamic but also helps identify any challenges early so that solutions can be introduced a lot earlier. A lot of time can be saved, making the processes more efficient too.

2. Empowerment

Every single individual needs to feel supported and guided throughout their career. The best way to do this is through check-ins and by initiating conversations to understand how every single team member is doing. And no, I do not mean a monthly feedback session, these conversations need to be ongoing and daily because work tends to be hectic and not everyone will remember the challenges they have undergone two or three weeks ago. Leaving any challenges or issues unnoticed or unresolved can have a negative long-term effect on the team as these issues will reoccur until they become bad habits. Which is something everyone wants to avoid.

3. Understanding
Being able to understand different nationalities and backgrounds goes a long way as it creates a deeper connection with everyone. A higher level of respect is introduced where everyone feels welcome and like they belong. This is especially important since hotels become temporary homes to multiple individuals during their travels and the slightest honest mistake could offend someone if there is no knowledge about their culture or customs. Having an open mind by understanding others is what makes a huge difference because people want to feel secure like they are at home.

4. Equality
All ideas and suggestions to improve work-life balance and processes should be encouraged from every single individual no matter what team they are part of or what position they have. This not only encourages different perspectives but also makes

colleagues feel heard and seen. When people feel heard and seen they are more likely to become vocal about their visions and perspectives. Additionally, it also teaches everyone that all guests should be treated fairly, and they will start speaking to all guests from their hearts.

Speaking about equality brings me to the second side of the coin – treating guests fairly and offering equal opportunities. This is not a topic that delves into equality based on nationality, religion, or gender, but rather equality for all individuals. So, what do I really mean? I am referring to offering equal opportunities and experiences for all guests because I believe that currently, we are not doing enough in that aspect. Mainly, I am referring to offering resources and services to increase accessibility and ease for people of determination because everyone should be able to experience the comfort of travel and being on vacation without any stress. According to the world health organisation (WHO) Over 5% of the world's population – or 430 million people – require rehabilitation to address their 'disabling' hearing loss. Those numbers are significantly high and rising. The hospitality industry should adapt to offer the highest level of ease for those who are deaf and hard of hearing. When looking around I noticed not all hotels offer sign-language training for their employees and this makes it difficult for those who are deaf to communicate.

Contrary to popular belief, not all individuals who are deaf can read or write in English, which is known to be a universal global language. This makes it harder for individuals who do not speak English as their first language to communicate when travelling. Being able to speak to someone in sign language makes them more confident in the decisions they make when travelling and it creates a greater level of trust. People are also instinctually drawn to connecting with one another and being able to communicate, so finding a hotel that offers communication through sign language will make guests feel a lot more welcome, cared for and happy. This additional crucial gesture adds another level of ease.

Before I delve into how hotels can become more accessible to deaf people, I would like to share with you the story of how I originally learned sign language. It all started when I was young. I previously mentioned how I used to start developing small business ventures in my free time after school to help my parents by providing an extra source of income. It might have seemed like that was all I ever did, however, I would also have a couple of free afternoons once I finished school. During those days when I wasn't selling soft drinks by the side of the road or selling vegetables at the market, I would spend time with my relatives. I would mostly spend time with my great-uncle from my mother's side, who cannot hear and speak at all. It was during my free afternoons and evenings with him that I learned how to speak using sign language. We would both spend time feeding, playing, and taking care of his pigeons. On top of his house, he built a huge pigeon house where he housed 50 to 60 pigeons. It was always a lot of fun to spend time together because we would let the pigeons fly freely and they would circle above the house. Some of them would also do flips whenever I would whistle or make a specific sound. The more noise I made, the greater number of flips we would see. It brought a lot of joy for both him and me. We were able to enjoy the simple things in life together. After an hour or two, the pigeons would suddenly come back to their house. It was incredible to see how someone who does not talk, who cannot hear, raise so many pigeons. He really understood the pigeon's feelings, and what they needed. Before spending time together, I did not understand sign language, but the more time we spent together, the more I learned. I would look at his gestures, hand movements and what he would point at to learn the different words and sentences. Sometimes his mouth would move, but there would be no sound, so I mostly relied on analysing the body language. The time we spent together really helped me understand people's emotions, how they feel and what they truly mean merely by observing what they were communicating with their body language. It took me about a month or two to learn and fully understand sign language to the point where we were able to crack jokes and laugh together with tears running down our faces. We were also very similar back then because he was also the type of person who was very eager to learn how to turn one dollar into two dollars. He decided to sell the birds at the market, and I would go support him in this venture by being his translator. I used to communicate and translate for him there. He was really happy to be making a bit of money on the side. I recently realised how important it is for us to create this space and inclusion for deaf people because they are not any different from us. They have a lot of great feelings like love, compassion, energy, and passion. Many of them see like as a beautiful source of happiness, they accept who they are and live life to the fullest. I learned so much from him in that regard and a lot of the learning was without talking, just by looking at the personality, the different feelings that emerged, and how people responded or acted. This helped me throughout my career because I could understand the people differently and truly see how they felt past the pretence.

Multiple people at the different hotels I worked at were surprised to see that I was able to communicate with the guests in sign language. Whenever someone needed any extra communication support, I would be ready to assist and help them. I used to explain to them how I learned to speak, and the biggest reward was their wide smiles, knowing that they had someone to talk to and rely on for accurate information.

So how can we as the hotel and tourism industry become more accessible to deaf people and what effect does that have on them? Firstly, three main benefits arise from hotel personnel being able to communicate in sign language to guests.

1. Memorable experience

Whenever people travel to a new country or when they take time off, they do so for multiple reasons. They are looking to relax, spend time with family, discover a new place, travel with their friends, or they are just generally aiming to recharge their batteries after a long time of working hard. One main aspect that links all these different reasons together is the desire to create memories and cherish new experiences. Whenever we travel to another country, language barriers can get in the way of creating smooth experiences which can taint some memories with negativity. Communication becomes a barrier for deaf individuals when they are unable to communicate with staff members at hotels to get travel advice or general information about best practices. Integrating sign language within a hotel should not be seen as an extra level of care or bonus step, because it is the standard way that certain individuals speak. When people are welcomed into a hotel by someone who can communicate through sign language it creates a memorable experience because the family knows they can rely on the management to make sure all their needs are met and fulfilled. It makes people feel cared for, heard and ultimately special.

2. Ease and convenience to navigate a new place
Whenever we travel to a new place, popular touristic places can often be found online, and it is easy to research places to visit. However, the smaller details such as unique places that are loved by locals, the restaurant that serves authentic, traditional food, and the places where you can shop for the best souvenirs (which are not incredibly expensive like in tourist hot spots), that's the additional information that makes a difference when travelling. There is no better guide than a person who lives and works in the country that you are visiting. It is easy for anyone to walk up to someone at a café or on the street to ask them about those details when they can communicate verbally and through a language that they both have in common. The way greater ease and convenience can be introduced to deaf people is by being able to communicate these answers through sign language or even touristic videos that communicate in sign language that can be accessed through the hotel's website. Being able to speak to the hotel management about the best time to visit specific touristic places, what hidden gems the city has to offer and even tips on how to best travel from place to place makes it easier to plan the day while making room for more authentic experiences.

3. Greater trust and lower anxiety

As with every trip that involves travelling to a new country or place, there is this heightened feeling of excitement as you expose yourself to new experiences and the anticipation of building special memories. However, at the same time, there is also a feeling of fear because now more than ever, there are lots of unknowns. As we navigate through the next few years, the COVID-19 virus still heavily influences travel plans, travel restrictions and regulations are constantly changing. It is difficult for everyone to get the latest updates and information when it comes to travelling, and it can prove to be even more difficult for everyone else. Sometimes the news of a lockdown or a curfew is announced in cities before it is announced to the entire country and globally. Being able to communicate with the hotel management and being kept up to date becomes extremely important during crucial moments as these; it can determine whether someone gets stuck in a country or if they can travel in time to go back home. That is precisely why hotel colleagues can make a huge difference to guests by being able to communicate the latest updates as soon as they find out from trusted news sources and governmental entities. Not all news channels that report breaking news have the option to watch the news in sign language or the option to read subtitles. Communicating this information can help build greater trust between the staff members and the guests, which will overall lower their anxiety and stress levels when travelling.

So how can we become the living GPS for deaf people? How can we make information more accessible and every single stay at our hotel memorable for a guest that has a hearing impairment? There are three main ways we can start making a difference and pushing for change within this hospitality industry.

1. Compulsory training

Introducing compulsory sign language training where hotel colleagues are taught the basics of communication. This can include being able to answer the frequent questions that anyone would ask during their stay at a hotel in a country they have never visited. One way to start is being able to introduce information about transport, places to visit, restaurants, and timings for different events that are taking place during their stay which the guests might be interested in. This training should be sponsored by the hotel as a talent investment to strengthen the workforce's skills and capabilities. Sufficient courses should be introduced throughout the year to improve the level of communication and refresh people's memory since they might not necessarily communicate in sign language every day.

2. Upgrade on-demand content

In every level of tourism, we need to start creating a customer program that includes sign language – covering what they would like to see because people don't just want to see pictures, they also want to gain knowledge from short videos. This includes explaining the main facilities, programs and events that surround the hotel. Even short videos about the different taxi prices and the taxi companies that they should trust so that they do not get scammed. This problem does not exist in the UAE, however, in some other countries, it is a very huge problem that multiple tourists face. The inclusive videos could be viewed for free using the hotel room's TV service or through the hotel's dedicated section on their website. These touristic videos can cover multiple topics about the country that the guests who are visiting are interested and all of it would be using sign language. The content would mainly show other people in the different touristic places explaining the best timings, routes, directions, and ways to make the most of that experience. Individuals who are interested in learning more about the culture and history can view videos that go in-depth about the country's traditions and historical aspects. Cuisine can also have a separate video segment where the top dishes of specific restaurants are recommended. Offering diverse content on-demand for anyone to watch as they take a break during their busy day of exploration adds value. I do not know a single hotel that offers this type of service. Not only does this create an inclusive environment for guests but it promotes the country they are visiting. Small, locally-owned businesses can be given exposure through this process as tourists love to be part of authentic experiences in a country that they are visiting for the first time.

3. More conversations – what is travel to them
Everyone faces different problems when they travel or when they go to a hotel. We can begin to understand what issues deaf people face by understanding them. This is why it is important to reach out to them and find out what aspects of their booking, travel and interaction process with the hotel can be improved. Are there any areas in which we are lacking that we may not be aware of? This is exactly how we can start learning more and opening the floor for conversation. This can also be done through feedback and making sure every single person who visits the hotel can describe their experiences. A focus on what can be done even better is pivotal so that future guests can benefit from even better services.

That was we can work towards giving them the kind of facilities, services and programs which are suitable for them – we can provide the one-stop-shop which includes a seamless process from the booking stages, until the time they see the city, and so on. Making everything easy is the main goal. Everyone loves to travel, take time off and enjoy themselves. We are the ones who need to adapt to better fit their needs.

Everything I mentioned is extremely powerful. So what does the big picture look like when everything that was mentioned is applied versus when it is not applied? Let's imagine that the guest has just arrived: They are standing in the lobby waiting for their turn to check-in. In the meantime, they are welcomed with a flower bouquet, QR code is shared with them. This QR code leads them to a platform that includes all the different informational videos that were mentioned and the contact details of the person who can speak sign language, letting them know that they'll be there for them 24/7. Being able to provide the telephone number of someone they can converse with over WhatsApp instead of going downstairs to the reception to ask them any questions they might have makes it easier for them. The only means of communication for deaf people is through sign language and writing down information – picking up the phone to make a quick call does not work. This is why this added WhatsApp service is the perfect way to add another layer of convenience.

It is amazing how humans can learn. When I learned English, it was not just from school, it was mainly by interacting with people when I was working, by talking to different nationalities, being curious about their upbringing, culture, and their life stories. It was the same with sign language, the constant interaction with my relative helped me get better and better at expressing myself and learning that form of communication. I always say and think that all life experiences, whether positive or negative, have a powerful effect on us all and it all depends on what we make of those experiences that will determine our level of success. It is the mindset that we carry during our day-to-day activities.

8

LAST FEW WORDS

This book may have been my first one, however, the ideas and the desire to create it have been brewing in my heart for fifteen years. My main wish is that whoever picks up this book and reads it feels inspired to take a step forward. You might be wondering, "A step forward, but what direction are you talking about"? There are multiple directions that I would like everyone to take a step towards and they do not all necessarily have to be at the same time. However, they can always change. It might be taking a step towards the direction of self-understanding. Where you finally understand who you are, why you make the decisions that you do daily, the reasoning behind the events that upset or trigger you and the purpose in life that you truly wish to pursue. This direction can lead you to a higher understanding of yourself which can ultimately heal old parts of you that have suffered in the past. That's the first step in gaining greater emotional intelligence because it ultimately changes how you interact with everyone; you begin to understand people better and you can spot the reasoning behind their negative behaviour. Another direction can be towards taking a risk such as following your true calling or adopting an unconventional mindset to come up with new, out-of-the-ordinary solutions. In so many industries we see calculated decisions being made and some people believe that these are the decisions that give you the best results. They seem like risk-free decisions, however, some of the best results within the hospitality industry are the ones that are achieved based on our heart's instinct. That is even more true now because the pandemic has really cut people off emotionally and many of us have had to resort to communicating, interacting, and socialising online. Our emotions and feelings can truly guide us into making decisions that ultimately make people happier. This is the first step towards giving passionate, talented, and hardworking individuals a chance to prove themselves even if they do not have that shiny diploma to back them up. I want to see more recruiters in the hospitality industry searching for individuals with emotional intelligence and passion. I also want to see more people taking a step towards being there for someone in need. That could be a student who is eagerly looking to learn from an expert, it could be your colleague who is going through some tough times, or it could be your neighbourhood janitor who is not having a great day. Our ability to help someone is amplified because once we help a person, they continue the cycle. That person begins to realise the impact the power of support has, and they pass on this support to a couple of people in their daily lives. When we look at lending a helping hand to young students and graduates, we really need to remember how hard it was for us when we first started. Nothing made sense, it was stressful, and we panicked a lot. Now, in the present, we can instil confidence, impart knowledge, and share our own stories that were filled with mistakes, struggles and eventual success. So why shouldn't we if we are able to? Our time as leaders will not last an eternity and that is why it is so crucial to prepare the young generation for their future. There are no better people to learn the ropes of life, work, and balance than from the people who have compiled years and years of experience.

If you are a leader who believes in the same, and you are reading this right now, I want us to connect. The online mentor's academy and bank of knowledge is something I want us all to start working towards. If you are a student or a graduate, and you have followed the advice in this book, I want to hear how it was able to help you! In the long term, I plan on impacting the world and continuing to support the new generation by giving them confidence in themselves, mentoring them, and showing them that they are talented in their own unique way. We all are, and we should never strive to be like anyone else. I hope that the stories that I have shared with you inspire you to start living your life differently than you currently are. There is a lot more that I want to share, and I will in the future. As the hospitality industry is constantly changing, we all need to continue adapting with an open mind. As we undergo multiple changes, I will continue to share my new ideas and visions with everyone so that we can all march towards a brighter and more compassionate future.

TESTIMONIALS

Rikhsibay is a breath of fresh air! He brings in-depth knowledge and lots of experience within hospitality through his role. His passion to deliver excellent service to his guests and partners is evident; he holds them at the heart of any decision and recommendation. He has a vibrant personality and is a huge asset to his team or any team he works with. His friendly nature makes him personable, and he is also extremely driven to succeed at anything he sets out to achieve. Simply put, Rikhsibay is a connoisseur of the hospitality industry. The Dubai Hotel Industry needs people like him to turn things around in rough times! Top professional, top bloke!

Samer Alloush
Group Commercial Director BNC Publishing

Rikhsibay is a very positive person; he cares about his work and takes the time to do it correctly. He is bubbly, outgoing, and has a great sense of humour. He is willing to help anyone in need and when he is in, he is all in. Rikhsibay is confident in himself and has good leadership qualities. He is able to keep calm and level-headed whenever he is in stressful situations. He is someone who can relate to anyone and any culture and background, which allows him to make very personal connections with everyone he meets. He is an honest and hardworking individual who is usually busy and likes to pursue his goals wholeheartedly. Moreover, he is an extremely determined person. No matter what, he will push through limitations and adversity to try and get what he wants and what is best for himself and those around him. Beyond that, he is extremely compassionate and kind and will do everything and anything for others.

Rehab Khalaf
Chief Human Capital Officer

Immaculate, detailed, knowledgeable and above all, incredibly passionate towards guest and staff satisfaction in a way that many hoteliers can only wish to be. I had the privilege of working with Rikhsibay at Dubai, which is evidently one of the finest hotels in the region, not because of the hardware but because of the immense effort that Rikhsibay has put in his daily role as an great leader. He is a person who leaves no stone unturned to find opportunities that can create an even greater guest experience. Rikhsibay infects those around him with his genuine desire to ensure that every guest need is anticipated, and at many times, exceeded.

Peter Avram
General Manager/Managing Avani Middle East

I have known Rikhsibay for almost twenty years and have always been impressed by his dedication, style, and attention to detail. Knowing that he was in charge of the operation meant that I could focus on more strategic issues because he always ensured a high standard of guest experience and satisfaction. He is dedicated to training and developing those around him and is an example to all of us in this regard. I wish him all the best and look forward to seeing his career develop further.

James Young MBA, FIH
Vice President Resource Planning and Development
WMC Group Vietnam

I met Rikhsibay in 2004 when I visited the Hotel Dubai to prepare for a series of seminars I was presenting. These events were a bit different and very demanding. They required flexibility, timeliness, precision, and a willingness to quickly and properly manage many unusual requests. Several other hotels had fumbled those tasks and had left me feeling uneasy about working with new venues and people. Rikhsibay was assigned to manage the operations of my meetings. From the beginning, he was not only unfazed by my requirements, but also embraced the challenge. Rikhsibay actually promised me that I would not find a hitch during the whole week. Led by him, the banquet team delivered flawlessly. During the event, I watched him operate and interact with workers and customers, and it was clear to me that this young man was a natural hotel operator. And by that, I do not mean a schmoozer with fine manners and a slick tongue. I mean a true hotelier: a leader that is effective, efficient, and reliable while remaining warm and friendly. I call those rare individuals "21st Century Hoteliers". Rikhsibay was always eager to learn and grow, seeking my guidance on such matters and applying it. During the next five years, and through several more meetings that he managed with equal success, I watched him grow as a manager, a leader, a student of our industry and – fortunately for me – as a friend. We have stayed in touch through the years, and it has not been surprising to see him rise through management and to see him get bigger and better assignments. A solid friend, a devoted father, a gentleman, and a 21St Century Hotelier. I do not write these terms lightly, though, in Rikhsibay's case, they come easily.

Rey Alcocer
Managing Partner at HSG
Solutions Group

I have known Rikhsibay for many years from the time he started his career in Dubai. He can be very proud of what he has achieved. He is proof that you can achieve big things if you have the right recipe. This recipe only has a few ingredients, and these include an ability to set achievable goals, honesty, hard work, lots of passion and one hundred per cent commitment. The next step is to make sure all resources and equipment are on hand and well respected. This recipe always works, and I can see that Rikhsibay adheres strictly to this recipe. Well done, and congratulations on your achievements. Stay on track and you will achieve a lot more.

Uwe Micheel
Guild President
Emirates Culinary Guild

AUTHOR'S BIO

Rikhsibay Tursunov is a highly motivated and passionate professional with over 25 years of experience in the hospitality industry working with luxury hotels. Before becoming a well-known individual with high emotional intelligence, he was merely a little boy in the village who was trying to provide for his family at the young age of fourteen. Trying multiple business ventures – like selling vegetables in the bazaar and Samsa at the animal market – helped him learn the true meaning of patience, perseverance, discipline, and genuine communication through connection. Now, emotional intelligence, empathy and understanding are the three main pillars that drive his leadership style. Over the years, Rikhsibay's communication skills and friendly personality have brought together multiple teams by creating an amicable, open, and reliable working environment for all. His eagerness towards mentoring the younger generation and empowering employees to grow stems from his lack of mentors when growing up. This is why, presently, Rikhsibay is constantly looking for new ways to share his knowledge, experience, and advice with anyone interested so they can have someone to turn to for guidance. The accomplished, results-driven business leader from the Luxury Hotel & Leisure sector is now working towards sharing his experience and knowledge of creating a comfortable, efficient, and lively work environment.

www.ingramcontent.com/pod-product-compliance
Lightning Source LLC
Chambersburg PA
CBHW022043160426
43209CB00002B/53